creative COLLAGE
for Scrapbooks

Kelly Angard

Fresh and Fun Techniques for Layering

MEMORY MAKERS BOOKS

Denver, Colorado

AUTHOR AND ARTIST *Kelly Angard*

MANAGING EDITOR MaryJo Regier

ART DIRECTOR Nick Nyffeler

PHOTOGRAPHER Ken Trujillo

ART ACQUISITIONS EDITOR Janetta Abucejo Wieneke

CRAFT EDITOR Jodi Amidei

GRAPHIC DESIGNERS Jordan Kinney, Jeff Norgord, Robin Rozum, Melanie Warner

CONTRIBUTING PHOTOGRAPHERS Lizzy Creazzo, Camillo DiLizia, Jennifer Reeves

EDITORIAL SUPPORT Jodi Amidei, Karen Cain, Amy Glander, Emily Curry Hitchingham, Dena Twinem

Memory Makers ® Creative Collage For Scrapbooks
Copyright © 2006 Kelly Angard
All rights reserved.

Published by Memory Makers Books, an imprint of F+W Publications, Inc.
12365 Huron Street, Suite 500, Denver, CO 80234
Phone (800) 254-9124
First edition. Printed in the United States.
10 09 08 07 06 5 4 3 2 1

Library of Congress Cataloging-in-Publication Data

Angard, Kelly, 1964-
    Creative collage for scrapbooks : fresh and fun techniques for layering / by Kelly
Angard.-- 1st ed.
        p. cm.
    Includes index.
    ISBN 1-892127-58-X
        1. Photograph albums. 2. Scrapbooks. 3. Photocollage. 4. Artists' books. I. Title.

TR501.A54 2005
745.593--dc22

2005053875

Distributed to trade and art markets by
F+W Publications, Inc.
4700 East Galbraith Road, Cincinnati, OH 45236
Phone (800) 289-0963

ISBN 1-892127-58-X

Distributed in Canada by Fraser Direct
100 Armstrong Avenue
Georgetown, ON, Canada L7G 5S4
Tel: (905) 877-4411

Distributed in the U.K. and Europe by David & Charles
Brunel House, Newton Abbot, Devon, TQ12 4PU, England
Tel: (+44) 1626 323200, Fax: (+44) 1626 323319
E-mail: mail@davidandcharles.co.uk

Distributed in Australia by Capricorn Link
P.O. Box 704, S. Windsor NSW, 2756 Australia
Tel: (02) 4577-3555

Memory Makers Books is the home of *Memory Makers*, the scrapbook magazine dedicated to educating and inspiring scrapbookers. To subscribe, or for more information, call (800) 366-6465.
Visit us on the Internet at **www.memorymakersmagazine.com**

This book is dedicated to some very special people that I am blessed to have in my life. To those who helped me see the fruit…

…to my amazing editor, MaryJo Regier—for planting and nurturing the seeds…

kept telling me that it was within my reach…

…to my special girl, Rachel—for your helpful hands and heart and very inspiring spirit…

…to Jake—for sharing your magic and leaving me sweet notes on my desk…

…and held the ladder steady so that I could reach out and grasp it.

…and especially to David, my love—for doing whatever it took to make my dream, our dream.

Thank you just isn't enough.

YOU'VE got to go OUT on a LIMB sometimes BeCause that's where the FRUIT is…

Table of Contents

3

68-91

Under the Surface

Chapter

4

92-117

Image Is Everything

Chapter

BLOOM
where you're planted

Introduction:
Evolution of an Artist

There are very few times in our lives when we have one of those real defining moments, when we're able to stop what we're doing and say to ourselves, "This is it! This is one of my dreams!" For me, right now is one of those moments. Writing this introduction—the beginning of this book—is actually a destination: a collage of a lifetime of moments, experiences, disappointments, dreams and goals.

It should be easy to put a date on when I started on this artful journey, but I can't. It's much more than a date when I started scrapbooking, or even loved creating art. It started the first time I knew I could make a mark on a piece of paper...the first time I held scissors in my hand and cut jagged edges. The first time I created anything. I don't have a conscious memory of those moments, but I'm sure the wonder and amazement was there then as it still is now.

During the process of putting this book together, I looked back at my first scrapbook pages and my first page *Memory Makers* published (back in 1998!). The scrapbook industry, and *Memory Makers*, was in its infancy, yet showed so much promise. Suddenly, a new form of expression and thought captivated the art and craft worlds, allowing each of us the opportunity to create our own personal history books no matter one's artistic level. The enduring message behind scrapbooking echoed the importance of family, memories and moments. And it spoke loudly to what we all want as mothers, sisters, daughters, friends and artists: a way to tell our stories, record our journeys and define our destinations.

Look at how far we've come—all of us! From the first time you picked up scissors or held a crayon in your hand to your first scrapbook page to now. From the first issues of *Memory Makers* when all there was to work with (or so we thought) was colored cardstock, die cuts and stickers—to now. Because the "now" for each of us is a culmination of moments, experiences, disappointments, dreams and goals, too.

So stop and enjoy this moment for yourself, and know that every time you create a layout, express yourself in journaling or complete a roll of photographs, you are building upon the collage of memories that will bring you to your destination.

Enjoy!

Kelly

Kelly Angard, Author and Artist
CREATIVE COLLAGE FOR SCRAPBOOKS

Collage Redefined

What do you think of when you hear the word *collage*? Do you think of it as an art technique? Or do you think of it as a type or style of art?

Whichever way you think of collage...you're right! Collage is both; it is a type of art as well as a way of creating art. The duality of collage keeps the door of creative possibility open for anyone to walk through—whether you're an illustrator, painter or scrapbook artist.

The word *collage* is derived from the French words "papiers colle" which means "pasted papers." This 20th-century art form, introduced by Picasso, revolutionized the art world by going beyond the limits of traditional painting. The introduction of the canvas as a surface to build and layer upon pushed art beyond the ordinary and provided unlimited and infinite possibilities.

While other traditional styles of art—such as impressionism or renaissance—are defined by a certain look, collage art is not. Collage, like life, is always changing and evolving. It is reflective of the artist and the world in which it is created.

So, collage can be whatever the artist wants it to be. It can be your art. You decide what you want it to be: It can be a collage of techniques, a collage of elements, a collage of words or a collage of something else. Explore the possibilities and give collage a new definition...yours.

Mixed-media collage invites a curious mind to wonder and marvel at what lies in between its mysterious layers.

The beauty of collage: Colorant, texture and image meld into a single element.

A collage of themed stickers (Flair Designs) is embossed on a photo album cover.

A new twist to traditional assemblage: Dimensional school elements and keepsakes are assembled inside sliced foam core windows.

The simple layering of monochromatic patterned papers creates a colorful and hypnotic background.

An example of the duality of collage: Torn vellum and patterned papers, called dechirage, are collaged together into a realistic image.

Types of Collage

ASSEMBLAGE	Combination of three-dimensional objects glued to a surface
BRICOLLAGE	Combining odds and ends to collage
DECHIRAGE	Torn or distressed paper collage
DECOLLAGE	Removing, ungluing or otherwise subtracting materials from the collage
DECOUPAGE	Cut-paper collage
FEMMAGE	Collage art and traditional craft done by women, frequently fabric-oriented
FROISSAGE	Crumpling or creasing collage materials
FROTTAGE	Rubbing a design onto collage materials from a textured surface
FUMAGE	Exposing dampened collage materials to surface candle smoke
MIXED MEDIA	Any combination of mediums with collage
MONTAGE	Combining collected or processed images
PHOTOMONTAGE	Collage of glued photographs or cutout photos

Basic Tools & Supplies

Who doesn't love getting new supplies? We may laugh at how much guys love their power tools and hardware, but in truth, we scrapbookers are no different. There's something mystical about creative supplies; it must be just in knowing that a new tool or supply is going to help us do what we love to do even better than we did before!

The supplies I've assembled below are used to create the wide range of techniques taught in this book. Most of these supplies are ones that I turn to time and again for a variety of uses. Golden's acrylic gloss, matte and gel mediums, for example, are superb adhesives as well as acrylic paint mediums. And watercolor pencils and crayons can be used either wet or dry, eliminating the need to purchase standard watercolors. Look around your own supply closet and substitute where you can, or get together with a few friends and spend a few hours experimenting with each other's tools and supplies before buying new ones.

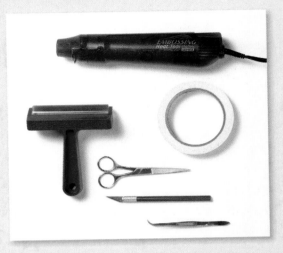

White artist's tape is less sticky than regular masking tape so it doesn't ruin cardstock when removed. Make sure to have a craft knife on hand and a supply of extra blades; once you get used to working with this tool, you'll wonder how you ever did without it.

Tools I Can't Create Without

Wax paper is a great palette for paint and ink; just toss in the trash when you've finished. Plastic palette knives can be used for spreading, mixing and burnishing. I find that I can never have enough sandpaper or paintbrushes in a variety of shapes and sizes on hand.

- Artist's tape
- Brayer
- Craft knife + blades
- Embossing gun
- Fixative spray
- Miscellaneous liquid adhesives
- Nonstick sheet

- Paper towels
- Repositionable adhesive
- Sandpaper
- Small sharp scissors
- Spritzer bottle filled with water
- Tracing paper
- Transfer paper

Everyday Tools I Love

A small quilting iron (Clover Needle-craft) comes in handy if you like to work with fabric or do iron-on image transfers. I also use mine to melt colorful wax crayons into beautiful and interesting designs. A heat tool (Walnut Hollow) with changeable tool points is always plugged in at my art table, usually with the craft knife or the stencil point for engraving a photo.

- **Baby wipes**
- **Cosmetic sponges and cotton swabs**
- **Heat tool**
- **Quilting iron**
- **Spritzer bottle filled with rubbing alcohol**
- **Wood skewers or manicure stick**

Colorant Tools

I use paint pens in metallic and solid colors to outline, touch up or dress up an element in seconds.

- **Foam brushes**
- **Inkpads and re-inkers, variety of types and colors**
- **Paint pens**
- **Paintbrushes, variety of sizes**
- **Palette knife** (*plastic or metal*)
- **Watercolor crayons**
- **Watercolor pencils**

Acrylic Art Mediums

Acrylic art mediums such as light molding paste or regular gel medium are perfect for scrapbooking because they are firm enough to hold a shape but don't weigh heavy on the page. Both can be mixed with acrylic paint before applying or applied right out of the jar and then colored; keep in mind, however, molding paste dries an opaque white while the gel medium dries clear.

- **Acrylic gloss medium or GAC 100**
- **Acrylic matte medium**
- **Golden acrylic paints**
- **Golden gesso**
- **Light molding paste**
- **Soft gel medium**

How to Use This Book

This book is all about YOU! It was designed with you, the scrapbook artist, in mind. It is not a gallery of layouts, but rather a collection of creative techniques that can be integrated with any style of scrapbooking. It is a book that showcases, explains and demonstrates techniques so that you will be able to bring a more creative approach to your scrapbook art.

Essential Elements of Scrapbook Art

The Essential Elements of Scrapbook Art came to me while creating this book. The repetition of experimenting with a variety of colors and mediums allowed me to define the "essential elements" a scrapbook artist works with again and again. As such, the techniques in this book are divided into four categories that I see as essential to creating scrapbook art: Colorant, Texture, Image and Assemblage/Collage. I use "collage" in place of "assemblage" throughout the rest of this book because the basic steps of assemblage—a layering of items—is basic collage. Each of the four chapters contains layouts, illustrated techniques with step-by-step instructions, variations, creative ideas and design inspiration.

What is unique about this book is that each layout features four techniques—one from each of the four Essential Elements categories. Each layout and its featured techniques are presented together in the Essential Element Diagrams. These diagrams visually demonstrate the featured elements in two ways: Collaged into a layout and enlarged to show detail.

Techniques

Throughout the creation of this book, I was committed to looking at the techniques from a few different perspectives. I not only looked at them from an artistic standpoint, I looked at them from the different skill levels of scrapbookers or paper artists who might likely say, "I could never do this!" I made a conscious effort to work and rework, to write and rewrite the techniques and their accompanying directions so that anyone can do them with ease. Will your art look like mine? Maybe or maybe not. But, truthfully, it should look like yours, because it is yours.

Many of the techniques in the book fall into an unspecified category I like to call Perfectly Imperfect; these types of techniques don't require perfection to look great (see Perfectly Imperfect below). This doesn't mean that all the other techniques require "perfection" to look good, it just means that these are pretty foolproof. You will enjoy the process of learning something new if you don't have the pressure of perfection on you. Take a look at Helpful Hints for Technique Success (page 13) for some great guidelines. If you try a technique and don't think it's quite your style, your time has not been wasted because now you know what you don't like, which is as important as knowing what you do like, especially when it comes to defining your own personal style.

Individual style was also a key element I considered when it came to creating and assembling the techniques. Each technique is versatile enough to stand alone on a layout or be combined with others. The versatility of these techniques really shines when you look at them as creative options that can be mixed and matched with other techniques. Just because I've presented four techniques together in a layout doesn't mean they always have to be used together. Create your own combination of techniques by selecting one from each of the Essential Elements categories (see chart) and you will have a look that is uniquely your own.

Perfectly Imperfect Techniques

Altered Patterned Paper	Fractured Photos
Brayered Ink Effects	Painted Transparencies
Collagraph Prints	Sheer Layers
Distressed Corrugated Metal	Sparkling Surfaces
Dye Ink Wash	Stamped Paint Imprints
Embellished Fabric	Torn Paper Texture
Embroidered Photos	Transparency Montage

Essential Elements Diagram

Colorant	Texture	Image	Collage
Sheer Layers (background)	Embossed Tissue Paper	Charming Accents	Basic Photomontage

Helpful Hints for Technique Success

Assemble your supplies and read over steps and hints before beginning the technique. Pay attention to color combinations and relationships. If you don't have the exact same colors I used, don't worry. The family of color is not as important as the combinations and relationship between colors. If I've selected monochromatic blues, go ahead and try monochromatic reds, just make sure the colors are monochromatic. If I'm using pastel yellow and orange, and you only have pastel blue and green, go ahead and use them; the relationship between the colors is what is important.

Think in terms of threes. When it comes to learning a new technique, I say do it three times! You've already got your supplies out and are mentally ready to try something new, so give yourself three chances to succeed at a new technique.

If a technique has three steps to it, do the first step three times and then move on to the second step and do the same. The time it will take to do each step the second and third time is nothing compared to the amount of time it will take to start all over again if you're not happy with the result.

If you're learning a colorant technique, don't just take out one piece of cardstock. If you learned the technique easily, then you'll have a few extra pieces of beautifully painted cardstock that can be used for another project or swapped with a friend. By doing the steps three times in a row, you take the pressure off of yourself to do it perfectly the first time!

Colorant

Altered Patterned Paper
Brayered Mask Effects
Collagraph Prints
Dye Ink Designs
Faux Corrugated Metal
Grunge Brushing
Metallic Photo Effects
Patterned Paper Transfer
Reverse Stencil Mask
Sheer Layers
Stamped Paint Imprints
Transparent Glazes
Vibrant Lacquers
Watercolor Washes

Texture

Aluminum Accents
Architextural Images
Carved Cardboard
Colored Wax Scraffito
Dimensional Stamping
Embossed Stencil Designs
Embossed Tissue Paper
Encrusted Embellishments
Gel-Medium Imprints
Molding Paste Textures
Sparkling Surfaces
Textured Foam Core
Torn-Paper Texture

Image

"Charm"-ing Accents
Decal Image Transfer
Embellished Fabric
Embossed Photos
Embroidered Photos
Fractured Photos
Inked Photo Effects
Painted Transparencies
Photo Bleaching
Photo Engraving
Photo Transfers
Retro Duotone
Rub-On Transfers

Collage

Abstract Photo Collage
Basic Photo Montage
Collagraph Prints
Designing on the Grid
Dimensional Collage
Dimensional Decoupage
Layered Photomontage
Letter and Word Collage
Multiphoto Mosaic
Photo Illustration
Punched-Shape Collage
Realistic Object
Transparency Montage

You
Are What You
Layer

Chapter

I begin this book with the finished product: the collage. I start here because I believe that the whole is greater than the sum of its parts, whether it's about who we are or what we create. The sum of your parts—the essence of you—is so much greater than just the color of your skin, the texture of your hair or the image of yourself.

What does this have to do with collage and scrapbooking? Everything. Because every layout you create is a collage. It is a collage of your thoughts, memories and feelings as much as it is a collage of color, texture and image.

The process of piecing together the meaningful moments of your life is as exciting as it is insightful because you are not only piecing together a collage of experiences, you are assembling the layers of your life.

Colorant

Does the idea of working with tissue paper remind you of juvenile art projects or stuffed gift bags? Well, that's about to change after you experience the sophisticated side of tissue paper. Discover how easy it is to enhance cardstock or create a colorful collage of translucent layers.

Texture

The unexpected combination of embossed UTEE and crumpled tissue paper produces a wrinkled and bubbled texture that just begs to be touched. This technique is worth trying, even if it's just to experience its unique texture.

Image

What girl can resist the allure of collecting "charm"-ing embellishments? Create your own encased images with clear UTEE and metal-rimmed tags. You'll be amazed at how easy it is to make these faux glass photo charms.

Collage

I've simplified an important design principle for assembling a basic photomontage. This principle regarding size, or scale, translates to whatever type of art or craft you enjoy creating. I've found that sometimes less is more, especially when it comes to deciphering design principles.

Layout supplies not listed with a technique can be found on page 122.

Colorant
Sheer Layers
(background)

Texture
Embossed
Tissue Paper

Image
Charming
Accents

Collage
Basic
Photomontage

Colorant

Sheer Layers

I love making things that appeal to my sense of curiosity, which is why I am always looking for new ways to create translucent layers. Tissue paper is an incredibly versatile medium to work with, whether you're looking to add translucent color or texture (or both!) to your art without adding bulk.

Tissue paper becomes magically transparent when coated with acrylic gloss medium; colors and designs seem to effortlessly blend as if they were painted atop one another. If you've only got white tissue paper, stamp a mix of designs with permanent ink or stain it with dye re-inkers before tearing into pieces. Use this quick-and-easy technique to enhance plain tags or transform an outdated patterned paper.

Supplies: *Patterned paper (SEI); patterned tissue paper (Anthropologie); acrylic gloss medium or GAC 100 (Golden); foam brush*

VARIATIONS

1 Tear tissue paper into 3 to 4" pieces. Brush gloss medium over section of patterned paper. Randomly place torn pieces on wet gloss medium; overlap areas for more intense color.

Layer text tissue paper (7 Gypsies) over a coordinating patterned paper (Provo Craft).

2 Brush on a generous second coat of gloss medium and smooth out large wrinkles with fingers while wet. Set aside to dry.

Add style to striped patterned paper (Provo Craft) with a metallic harlequin tissue paper (DMD).

Texture

Embossed Tissue Paper

I used to love going to the fabric store as a little girl and walking by the bolts of fabric with my arm outstretched so that I could "feel" all the colors and patterns. Today, I still find myself reaching out to touch colors or designs that capture my eye and pique my interest; it's as though I can't fully appreciate what I'm seeing until I touch it.

I set out to create a texture for this layout that would capture the shine and luster of my puppy's coat. While I didn't quite achieve the suede look I was going for, I did like the unexpected outcome: a smooth yet uneven texture of shiny color. After adding a flash of metallic foil, I realized that this cool texture, like Buster, was hard to resist touching!

Supplies: *Acrylic gloss medium or GAC 100 (Golden); ColorBox brown ink pads (Clearsnap); Versamark watermark ink pad (Tsukineko); clear embossing powder (Stamp 'n Stuff); clear UTEE (Suze Weinberg); gold embossing foil, (Stampendous!); embossing gun; cardstock; white tissue paper; foam brush*

VARIATIONS

A vivid sunflower takes on a painterly effect after the applied tissue paper is inked and coated with pearl and clear UTEE. Make sure to spray inkjet photos with Fixative Gloss so inks won't run.

The sea sparkles with pearlescent effects...blue and beige inks define sea from sand. Enhance sea foam with pearl foil (Stampendous!).

1 Crumple white tissue; flatten but do not rub out wrinkles. Tear into 3 to 4" pieces. Brush a generous layer of acrylic gloss medium onto cardstock. Place crumpled tissue paper in wet acrylic medium; gently push into wet medium with brush, keeping as many wrinkles as possible. Set aside to dry before moving on to next step.

2 Rub brown ink pads over tissue paper texture; sprinkle clear embossing powder on top and set with embossing gun.

3 Rub watermark ink over texture; sprinkle clear UTEE and set with embossing gun. While UTEE is hot, press on gold embossing foil, waiting about 10 seconds before pulling off. Keep moving the embossing gun when setting embossing powder; tissue paper is delicate and prone to turning brown if overheated.

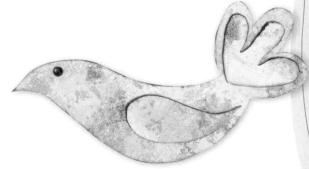

Pastel orange, yellow and lime green inks, a touch of green embossing powder and pearl foil (Stampendous!) blend together for a soft, impressionistic look.

Image

"Charm"-ing Accents

Add the allure of fashionable photo charms to your scrapbook page without having to solder metal or cut glass. An empty metal-rimmed tag becomes a ready-made frame for containing melted UTEE that gives the illusion of glass. Keep in mind UTEE hardens quickly; be prepared to work fast once you begin pouring. I suggest working on a nonstick surface such as a Teflon craft sheet or wax paper.

Try this technique to create encased minicollages, feature a decorative monogram or display inspirational words. Paint and embellish the metal rim before attaching a jewelry jump ring.

Supplies: *Metal-rimmed tags (Making Memories); clear UTEE (Suze Weinberg); melting pot (Ranger); gold paint pen (Krylon); craft knife; liquid adhesive; embossing gun; wooden skewer, paper piercing tool or large toothpick; water in spritzer bottle; jump rings*

Don't have a melting pot? No worries! Simply glue the metal frame over the image at the center of a large piece of paper. Apply a liquid adhesive over the image inside the frame. Quickly sprinkle a heavy application of UTEE onto glue inside metal frame; do not shake excess off. Carefully lift up and heat from underneath until the UTEE is melted. Sprinkle a second application of UTEE onto still warm UTEE; do not shake excess off. Heat again from underside. Repeat three or four more times, or until a thick, glasslike layer of UTEE is achieved.

1 Remove center of metal-rimmed tag with craft knife. Apply glue to back of tag frame; mount over image as shown.

2 Melt UTEE in melting pot. Pour UTEE inside of metal-rimmed frame working toward the center until it begins to overflow onto the metal rim. Quickly stick skewer in warm UTEE for jump ring hole; hold until enamel sets. Heat UTEE with embossing gun to even out lumpy areas or scrape from metal rim; set aside until cool. Use a wooden skewer or cuticle stick to move hot, liquid UTEE into place; scrape excess UTEE off the metal rim.

3 Turn tag over; spritz with water and gently rub with fingers in a circular motion to remove paper from back of tag. Have patience; you will need to repeat water spritz while rubbing until all the white paper is gone and you can see through the UTEE image. Add gold paint to back of tag and over the metal frame with gold pen.

VARIATIONS

Re-create the charm of a weathered windowpane; apply white acrylic paint to metal tag frame and lightly sand.

Two quick coats of acrylic paint (gold and red) on the metal tag frame add to the retro charm of the image.

Create a free-form golden nugget by pouring UTEE over image without a metal-rimmed tag frame. Apply UTEE one layer at a time until desired thickness is achieved.

Collage

Basic Photomontage

When it comes to creating a balanced collage, size does matter! Collage art can be chaotic when there is no clearly defined range of sizes, also called "scale." I could give you a lot of design principle mumbo-jumbo when it comes to explaining scale, but I'd rather simplify things by saying this: *think small, medium and large.*

Sounds simple, doesn't it? You really can't go wrong if you think small, medium and large when it comes to assembling a number of elements in a collage or layout. I re-sized the photos of my puppy's face so they would vary in size (scale). This allowed one of his faces (the largest) to stand out more than the other two, thereby creating a sense of depth and dimension.

Let's take this principle and apply it to a simple layout. Say, for example, you want to feature a large photo on your page, think small, medium and large. A large photo means that the other main elements (like title and embellishment) should be small- and medium-sized. To help demonstrate this principle in visual terms, take a look at the following layout examples.

"Something About Mary," page 23 (small title, medium embellishment, large photo) and "Alex," page 101 (small embellishment, medium photo, large title).

Start with a simple photomontage like this one, and then try your hand at a collection of patterned papers. When it comes to combining patterns, remember to think *think small, medium and large!*

Supplies: *Scissors*

1 Select a group of photos that has one large focal point (portrait, architecture, tree, etc.) in a variety of sizes. If you don't have a group of photos that would work, make two copies of one photo with a distinct focal point—the first 25 percent larger and the other 25 percent smaller than the original. Silhouette cut each focal point from the photo.

2 Place the images in order according to size, smallest to largest. Layer the images in a horizontal line in whatever order you find pleasing. Notice that the largest silhouette becomes the focal point of the three no matter where it is placed. Try layering the images vertically or in a cluster for a completely different look.

VARIATIONS

The adventurous spirit of a boy actually looks peaceful when assembled in a variety of sizes.

Patterned paper collections (Anna Griffin) are perfect for creating a design montage. The large graphic flower, cut from patterned paper, is layered over smaller scaled patterns.

Colorant

I'm telling secrets here, and this one is so worth the price of admission! When it comes to creating a stunning color wash, you've got to start with a great color combination.

Texture

Exposing the peeled layers and ribbed texture of cardboard opens up a realm of unique texture and embellishment possibilities. Carve out some time to transform a few layers of cardboard into a unique and colorful surface.

Image

Add a cool artistic element to your page with photo effects that dance somewhere between pop art and new-millennium technology. Don't worry if you're not into working with image-editing software; this photo effect can be created with a copier or a printer!

Collage

These torn-paper flowers give the illusion of a high-contrast, pop-art-inspired duotone. While the flowers may look complicated and detailed, the technique used to create them isn't. Besides, I've provided simple steps and diagrams that will have you painting with paper in no time!

Layout supplies not listed with a technique can be found on page 122.

THERE'S SOMETHING ABOUT

Mary

Colorant

Dye Ink Designs
(background)

Texture

Carved
Cardboard

Image

Retro
Duotones

Collage

Realistic
Object

Colorant

Dye Ink Designs

This funky and artistic background is a combination of a dye ink stain and a dye ink wash. Both are created with a brayer and dye re-inkers and together create a vibrantly colored background.

So, if the secret to creating beautiful stains and washes lies in selecting the right color combinations, what is the secret to selecting great color combinations? Use a resource!

That's right, a resource. The bottom line is that you do not need to know everything about color and design and layout to be a great artist. You just need to know where to find the answers to what you don't know! I use an online color tool called The Color Schemer whenever I need a little help with my color choices.

The Color Schemer (*http://www.wellstyled.com/tools/colorscheme2/index-en.html*) is a free online color generator which provides combinations for a color you select from the on-screen color wheel. This tool allows you to choose the type of combination, i.e., contrast, triad, analogous, etc., as well as the tone (jewel tone, pastel, etc.) and then presents a harmonious palette of colors (choose analogous for a color wash) in the blink of an eye. You'll be amazed at how quickly you'll learn foolproof color combinations while using this tool and will soon find yourself predicting the Schemer's choices.

Now that you've got the information you need at your fingertips, let's try the technique.

Supplies: Ancient Page dye ink re-inkers (Clearsnap); white cardstock (glossy or coated paper will produce a different effect); alcohol in spritzer bottle; brayer; gesso (white acrylic paint will work too); baby wipes; foam brush

VARIATIONS

I love this effect! The same dye-ink technique flows across glossy photo paper giving a whole different effect. Print photo first and then brayer ink; draw frame with gold paint pen (Krylon).

Drip dye inks (Jacquard Products) and draw design (Sharpie) on silk fabric for a luscious combination of colors.

Brayer a faux batik print by stamping the foam flower stamp with watermark ink before brayering tropical colors.

1 Select light-colored inks (Flamingo, Melon, Lime) to stain the cardstock. Randomly dot and scribble re-inkers on cardstock; lightly mist with alcohol spritzer four to five times. Quickly brayer back and forth to spread the inks. Repeat entire step; let dry. Note how an increased amount of ink and alcohol turns a stain into a wash.

2 Now you're going to apply a wash of color. Drizzle six to eight drops of all ink colors (add in the Turquoise and Neptune) on the cardstock. Hold the alcohol spritzer close to the cardstock and spritz four to five times, getting the cardstock wet. Quickly brayer back and forth. Repeat the process until you've covered the cardstock with a wash of inks. Speed drying time with a heat gun if you'd like.

3 Dip foam brush into gesso (or white acrylic paint); dab excess onto a paper towel to ensure a light application. Brush across cardstock three or four times with loose horizontal strokes. Grab a baby wipe and wipe over cardstock, partially removing and blending the gesso. Repeat this step with vertical strokes.

Texture

Carved Cardboard

I'm not quite sure what it was that prompted me to slice and carve into cardboard other than my curiosity. Its peeled layers and ribbed texture called to me until I began carving shapes, letters and designs. Then came the paints, fibers, beads, foil and more. I had great fun transforming a rugged piece of cardboard into something I didn't even recognize!

I'm not going to tell you that this is a quick technique, but I can say that the results are worth the time it takes. It is relatively easy if you are comfortable working with a craft knife. If you're not, don't worry; I've included a tip so you can get the look of carved cardboard without having to suffer through any detailed knife work.

***Supplies**: Transfer paper (Saral); 12 x 12" cardboard; pencil; craft knife; tweezers; small, pointed scissors*

Tips Turn cardboard as you carve instead of turning your hand. Make sure you've got a new blade in your craft knife. Practice on a separate piece of cardboard for confident craft-knife control.

Variations

Cardboard never looked so good! Camouflage a funky cardboard frame with carved letters and designs created with acrylic paints (Golden), image transfers, fibers and embossing foil (Stampendous!).

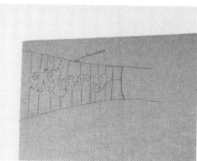

1 Transfer, draw or stencil letters onto cardboard. Slice along letter lines with a craft knife, cutting through first layer only. Do not press the knife all the way through to the back of the cardboard. Some areas will be easy to slice, while others will require an up and down sawing motion.

2 You will be carving the cardboard out from around the letters, so you will need to determine a carving area. Draw borderlines to determine carving area; slice along lines with craft knife. Create sliced sections for fast removal of cardboard layers; draw vertical lines from each letter's edge to the border line as shown in the photo. Slice over lines with the craft knife.

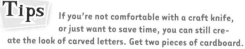

Carve out a place to feature woodland creatures. Follow the steps above. Print outline of animals on patterned paper and silhouette cut; mount over carved cardboard.

3 Now you're ready for the fun part: stick your craft knife (or tweezers) into the sliced letter outline; pull top layer of cardboard up and away from the letter. Grasp ribbed layer of cardboard with tweezers and pull up and away, leaving only the bottom layer of cardboard. Repeat until all of the layers in the carved area are gone. Tweezers are essential to remove small remnants of cardboard. Clean jagged edges with small pointed scissors as needed. Now you're ready to paint!

Tips If you're not comfortable with a craft knife, or just want to save time, you can still create the look of carved letters. Get two pieces of cardboard.

Draw, stencil, transfer or trace letters onto the one piece of cardboard; silhouette cut using sturdy scissors. Tear the top two layers from an area on the second piece of cardboard; mount cut letters in the torn-out section of cardboard using foam spacers.

Image

Retro Duotones

Yes, the 70s are back with a modern twist and the colorful fun of pop art! This retro influence translates well when it comes to photo art, and what better place to feature this look than on your scrapbook pages!

A duotone is a black-and-white photo that has a single color added to it. Believe it or not, you do not need to be a whiz with image-editing software to create the look of a duotone; a color copier will give you the same effect. Follow the equation and the steps below to create some fun duotone effects.

Use a spray vellum adhesive (Helmar) so the vellum will adhere firmly to the cardstock.

Black-and-white image + blue vellum + blue cardstock = duotone

Turn a color photo into a black-and-white photo either by color copier or scan and print. Print black-and-white photo onto blue vellum. Allow the ink to dry before touching it or placing anything on it. Coat the back of the vellum with a spray adhesive (this is important) and mount it on a piece of blue cardstock. Smooth the photo over the cardstock and voilà—instant duotone!

How easy was that? With a simple change of vellum or cardstock color, you can create a number of different tonal effects.

Monochrome   *Tritone*

Duotone   *Quadtone*

VARIATIONS

Play around with the contrast button on a copier or printer to create the funky foursquare below.

Monochrome—One color (black used above)
Copy or print black-and-white image onto plain vellum; mount on metallic (silver) cardstock for a luminescent effect.

Duotone—Two colors (black and yellow used above)
Copy or print black-and-white onto yellow vellum; mount on yellow cardstock.

Tritone—Three colors (black, yellow and blue used above)
Copy or print black-and-white onto blue vellum; mount on yellow cardstock.

Quadtone—Four colors (black, magenta, yellow and green used above)
Copy or print image in single color (magenta) onto yellow vellum; mount on green cardstock.

Collage

Realistic Object

Contemporary paper art meets the fine art of collage. Sounds impressive and looks complex, doesn't it? I love how a combination of layers can give the illusion of complexity when in fact the techniques to achieve the look are quite simple and basic.

The key to understanding and re-creating any type of complex art is to allow your mind to think in simplistic terms. For example, the flowers seen here are made by layering pieces of torn paper. You can so do that! In fact, you have probably already layered torn paper, just not into a realistic image.

For a project like this, I recommend using a Xyron adhesive machine for quick and easy assembly of torn paper strips.

COLOR VALUE (See step 1)

Think of color value as the shades of a single color, i.e., light, medium, dark. Defining an image's color values becomes easy after making a high-contrast color copy of the image because it blends some of the light and dark areas together making the definition between light and dark easier to define. Look for the lightest shade and the darkest shade of color first, and then look for the shades of color in between the two.

DEPTH VALUE (See step 2)

In simplistic terms, depth values are the foreground, middle ground and background. As a scrapbooker, you are probably familiar with these terms because your layouts begin with a background and then you layer the elements. The same is true here because the background flower is assembled first.

HINTS FOR EASY ASSEMBLY

· Which flower is in the foreground and which flower is in the background? Assemble background flower first.

· Which petals on a single flower are in the foreground and which petals are in the background? Assemble background petals of a flower first.

· How are the colors layered on each petal, i.e., which shade of pink is on top and which shade is on the bottom? Layer the petals starting with the background color first.

Supplies: *Pattern on page 120; adhesive machine (Xyron); colored paper; tweezers*

1 Copy or scan the image (page 120) to desired size; print or copy two color copies onto white cardstock. Mark one "reference" and the other "design." Define the four values of each color as I have. Select colored papers according defined values. Mark values and tape paper scrap to the reference copy.

2 Determine the foreground, middle ground and background of flowers and petals as described left. Mark on the reference copy; this will be a valuable guide when it comes to assembling the flower as a whole as well as the construction of each petal.

3 Apply adhesive to back of colored papers; randomly tear into small strips. Begin layering the background petals of the background flower; select torn strips that closely resemble the shape of a color value, but do not worry about matching the exact shape. You are going for a look, not an exact match. Mount layered petals right over the petals on the copy marked "design." How easy is that? Keep in mind that colored papers are easier to tear and layer than cardstock.

VARIATION

This technique easily translates a photo into a large-scale landscape; torn pieces of vellum and patterned papers are layered to re-create the beauty of a seasonal transition.

Tip Keep thinking in simplistic terms: look at your reference copy as a basic paint-by-numbers guide.

Colorant

I really like incorporating the unexpected into my art; adding a little "something-something" that says "wow" without overpowering the page makes for interesting and unique layouts. Follow the random thoughts and images that pop into your head when it comes to creating; you'll never know what kind of fabulous art you can create if you don't try!

Texture

Get ready for a new twist on an old decorative art technique—stenciling! Today's stencils look more like art than stenciling, with laser-cut designs ranging from sophisticated botanical imprints to modern ornamental flourishes that resemble architectural-relief motifs.

Image

Whether you're a big fan of embellishing with a needle and thread or not, this technique is not about perfectly embroidered designs; uneven and imperfect stitching adds unique charm and interest to a photograph.

Collage

Here's one of those techniques that looks a lot more difficult than it is. This abstract photo collage may look complicated, but it's not. If you can cut a design apart and reassemble it, you can do this!

Layout supplies not listed with a technique can be found on page 122.

Essential Elements Diagram

July 2002

Colorant
Faux
Corrugated
Metal

Texture
Embossed
Stencil Designs

Image
Embroidered
Photos

Collage
Abstract
Photo Collage

Colorant

Faux Corrugated Metal

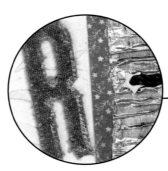

Portrait layouts are a great way to showcase a loved one's unique personality and characteristics. When it came to designing a portrait of my daughter, I knew that if I really wanted to represent "her" (i.e., "I don't wear dresses, Mom!"), I needed to create a look that was unique and feminine but certainly not frilly! While the photo definitely said "All-American" to me, the challenge was coming up with a feminine look that fit the theme. For some reason, corrugated metal came to mind, so I was left to figure out a way to get the look without adding bulkiness to the page or cuts to my hands.

Lucky for me, the hardware store held the answer. Thin, metal repair tape provided the metallic shine and flexibility I was looking for without the weight. After adding a few colorant and distressing techniques, the creative possibilities really began to flow. Follow the steps below and make sure you adhere the tape to a lightweight piece of paper, not cardstock, so that the crimper can give it a really good groove.

Supplies: *Metal repair tape (3M , Nashua); ColorBox chalk inkpads (Clearsnap); crimper (Fiskars); paper; sandpaper (fine or medium grain); cosmetic sponges*

VARIATIONS

A vintage-inspired symbol shines with glitter glue and rhinestones applied over two coats of white paint distressed with sandpaper.

① Cut electrical tape in random-sized lengths. Adhere to regular copy paper horizontally, vertically and diagonally as shown. Press all edges of the tape down with your fingers; smooth out as many wrinkles as you can.

② Distress tape by rubbing with sandpaper in all directions; push edges and corners down if they begin to lift. Lightly rub colored inkpads over tape for just a hint of color; blend with cosmetic sponge. Randomly sand inked areas.

Two coats of sanded acrylic paint reveal a dramatic heart.

③ Cut or tear into strips; feed through crimper.

Paint an Americana-inspired design using a basic shape stencil.

Texture

Embossed Stencil Designs

The art of reinventing and recycling things requires us to look at what we have with new eyes, whether we're talking about ourselves, our clothes or our art supplies. After pulling my collection of stencils from the closet, I realized how much the look of this decorative art has changed. Words like artistic, textured, graphic, sophisticated and ornamental describe today's stenciling, yet the simplicity of the technique has remained the same.

This white-on-white textured background won't take attention away from the other elements on the page and is as easy as spreading cake frosting. Acrylic mediums (see page 11) such as acrylic molding paste or gel medium can give a stenciled design sculptured style.

Look for some eclectic and contemporary stencil designs in the decorative painting or embroidery sections of your local craft or home/hardware store.

Supplies: *Decorative stencil (Delta); repositionable adhesive spray (Delta); light molding paste, pearl acrylic paint (Golden); palette knife; fine-grain sandpaper; foam brush*

Tip

For easy clean up, remove the molding paste from the stencil with a baby wipe before it dries!

VARIATIONS

A light and airy textured design (Delta) is enhanced with soft swooshes of ColorBox chalk ink (Clearsnap).

1 Spray stencil with repositionable adhesive; lay on cardstock. Spread a thick layer of molding paste over stencil with palette knife as if it were cake frosting. Lift stencil away and move to next area. For easy cleanup, remove the molding paste from the stencil with a baby wipe before it dries!

2 Create a smooth flat design by gently sanding with fine-grain sandpaper. Using a foam brush, paint over entire stencil and background with pearl acrylic paint.

Enhance patterned paper (Basic Grey) with a similar stencil design (Plaid). Apply creme paint (Golden) that blends with paper over dried molding paste; quickly wipe with a baby wipe to remove excess paint from paper. Rub inkpads (Colorbox chalk inks by Clearsnap) over raised areas.

A delicate laser-cut feather stencil (Stewart Gill) produced beautiful textured results with molding paste, embossing foil (Stampendous!) and metallic rub-ons.

Image

Embroidered Photos

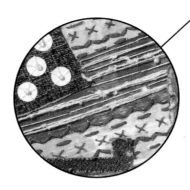

If you like working with textile notions such as fibers, fabric swatches, embroidery threads, beads and sequins, then this is the technique for you! If you're not that into stitching, I encourage you to try this technique because you won't be stitching a large area, just a few details here and there. Please know that this technique is not about perfectly embroidered designs (unless that is what you want); uneven and imperfect stitching adds to this technique's unique charm because there is something so loving and heartwarming about hand-stitched details (especially imperfect ones!).

Personalize your design with meaningful embellishments; I snipped a swatch of denim from an old pair of my daughter's jeans. It wasn't until after I had completed the stitched photo that I realized how much I liked the contrast between the photo surface and the soft threaded designs.

Supplies: *Photo strip (Creative Imaginations); sandpaper; denim fabric; sequins; seed beads; paper piercing tool; sewing needle; embroidery threads*

Tips • Look for photos that have bold lines and simple images; the flag's stripes provided clear boundary lines to stitch within.

• If you're not comfortable with jumping right in with needle and thread, make a few color copies onto cardstock; draw your ideas on the image and practice stitching.

• Lightly sand the photo before stitching. A light, distressed photo works well with the look of imperfect stitching, and fingerprints won't be as noticeable.

VARIATIONS

❶ Lightly sand photo with horizontal strokes. Mount fabric scrap with liquid adhesive; glue sequins and beads in place and let dry. Pre-pierce holes before stitching sequins and seed beads.

Hand-stitched details add warmth to a favorite winter-day portrait. Print photo on textured cardstock; stitch with fibers (Fiber Scraps). Mount patterned paper frame (A.W. Cute) with foam spacers.

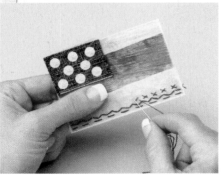

❷ Place photo on cutting mat; pre-pierce stitching lines with needle or paper-piercing tool so photo doesn't buckle when stitching. Stitch rows with a variety of stitches as shown.

Embroidery thread stitches and glass beads enhance the elegant details of a blooming flower.

Collage

Abstract Photo Collage

Here's a collage technique that will add instant artistry to your layout. This type of collage, called an Interval Collage, is created by cutting a design or image apart and putting it back together with a variety of elements—in this case, patterned paper. It is a great technique for a collection of patterned papers you're not sure what to do with.

The trick to making this technique easy is in the prep work, i.e., printing or copying the photo and abstract design onto patterned papers! When it comes to selecting patterned papers, make sure to include at least five light and minimally busy patterns or a few light solid colors.

I have simplified this technique by supplying the abstract pattern (see page 120). To prepare to create this type of collage, first size your photo and the pattern to 8 x 10". Scan and print or color copy photo onto six to eight coordinated patterned papers. Then, scan and print or color copy the design over the photos printed on the patterned papers. Print two copies of the photo and pattern on white cardstock; write "reference" on one and "design" on the other.

You are so ready to create this unique image design!

Supplies: *Abstract pattern on page 120; patterned papers (Flair Designs, Keeping Memories Alive, Scrappin' Dreams, Scrap Happy); pen; craft knife; liquid adhesive; embroidery thread; beads*

VARIATION

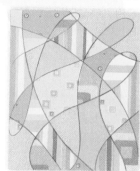

Try this technique with patterned paper (Provo Craft) collections and eliminate the embellishment step for a quick and stylish background.

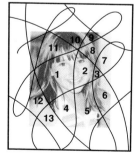    

1 Write numbers 1 to 13 in design sections on your "reference" copy as shown above. Select one of the patterned papers for section 1; assign another patterned paper to section 2 and so on until all five papers have been assigned a section. Try not to assign any of the same patterned papers to sections that are next to each other.

2 Using a craft knife, slice or cut out section 1 along borderlines. Do the same for each of the five sections; you should be cutting out one section per piece of patterned paper.

3 Take out the color copy marked "design." Mount each cut section over the corresponding area on the "design" copy. Don't worry if the border lines don't match up perfectly; we'll cover them up in step 5.

4 Repeat steps 1, 2 and 3 for sections 6 to 13. Assign all printed patterned papers to sections 6 to 13; make sure to repeat a few of the first five papers for consistency. Look to your reference sheet for guidance.

5 Apply liquid adhesive over black lines; press embroidery thread onto wet adhesive. String beads as you go and glue in place where lines intersect.

Colorant

Pump up the volume of color and shine with creative colored lacquers. The combination of re-inkers and glazing adhesives are sure to infuse your embellishments or images with a jolt of dimensional color.

Texture

At a time when everything old seems new again, tried and true techniques are resurfacing with a new twist. The simple act of tearing, cutting and layering paper creates subtle shadows and a texture that is reminiscent of contemporary and modern art.

Image

No matter how hard we try, our photos don't always turn out as we would like…but we still want to use them. This technique offers a creative way to feature a focal point, camouflage an unsightly background or add an unusual visual element to your layout.

Collage

The versatility of collaging with punched shapes knows no limits. Whether you choose to create a simple design or layer an intricate image, punched shapes become more interesting when they are assembled from an array of patterned papers.

Layout supplies not listed with a technique can be found on page 122.

Essential Elements Diagram

Colorant
Vibrant
Lacquers

Texture
Torn-Paper
Textures

Image
Fractured
Photos

Collage
Punched-Shape
Collage

Colorant

Vibrant Lacquers

If you haven't worked with crystal lacquer or Diamond Glaze as a colorant, then you're in for a real treat. While you probably know both products work wonderfully as clear dimensional adhesives, you may not have realized that they can also be used as dimensional colorants. Diamond Glaze and crystal lacquer can be mixed with alcohol inks or dye re-inkers to create vibrant, translucent colors.

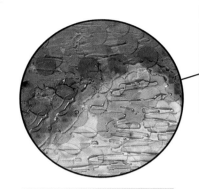

Supplies: *Diamond Glaze (JudiKins); dye ink (Clearsnap)*

Tips

Eliminate bubbles by placing crystal lacquer or Diamond Glaze upside down in a cup for 10 to 15 minutes prior to applying. Pop any bubbles that occur with a needle or safety pin while still wet.

VariaTions

1 Diamond Glaze/ Crystal Lacquer
To add colorant to Diamond Glaze, squeeze about a ½" circle of Diamond Glaze or crystal lacquer onto printed transparency.

Translucent colors (Diamond Glaze + dye ink) applied on the back of a purchased printed transparency (Creative Imaginations) adds colorful accents in seconds.

2 Drip two drops of alcohol or dye ink directly on the puddle of Diamond Glaze/crystal lacquer; blend and spread with a paintbrush. Too much of either kind of ink will prevent the Diamond Glaze/crystal lacquer from hardening. Note how the ink spreads into the Diamond Glaze or crystal lacquer in a tie-dye effect. Allow to dry before using.

before

after

Alcohol ink dripped onto wet Diamond Glaze spreads and blends by itself. Blast the mix with heat from an embossing gun, and watch the colors start to bubble. Once the heat is taken away, you've got a cool textured mix of color.

1 Color Crystal Laquer
To create seahorse tail, an image printed on inkjet transparency is enhanced with rows of blue and green crystal lacquer wavy lines and loose horizontal scribbles. Work from top to bottom so you don't accidentally rest your hand in wet lacquer. Set aside to dry for at least 20 minutes before mounting on page.

A colorless winter scene comes to life with a vibrant dye ink/Diamond Glaze mix. Sand photo before applying dye-ink and Diamond Glaze blend. Scratch into damp ink/lacquer with wooden skewer; let dry. Draw over tree branches with black fine-tip pen. Add a final coat of clear lacquer.

Texture

Torn-Paper Textures

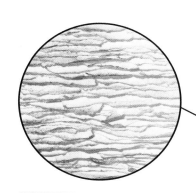

Even though the art of scrapbooking is not that old, I've noticed how the really good and simple tools and techniques have found their way back into our hands and onto our pages. Creating texture with torn paper is one of those basic techniques that is easy to learn and quite versatile when it comes to personal style. Its subtle presence is a nice contrast to the strong, geometric lines we are seeing so much of.

I like the fact that torn-paper techniques don't require perfection to look fabulous, and this technique is no different. Use plain white paper for elegant simplicity or use an old map for a visually interesting texture.

Supplies: *Colorbox chalk inkpads (Clearsnap); Versamark watermark inkpad (Tsukineko); rainbow embossing powder (Ranger); plain white paper; double-sided tape; heat gun*

VARIATIONS

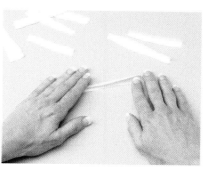

1 Tear white copy paper into ¾ x 5" strips. Fold each strip horizontally in half as shown. Tear paper strips with one continuous rip; trying to control a tear results in a choppy edge instead of a smooth, graceful tear.

The simplicity of torn and layered colors makes for a stunning background.

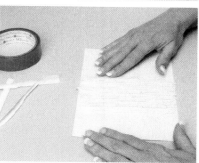

2 Adhere double-sided tape to cardstock. Mount first folded strip at the top of taped area, torn edge up. Layer rows from top to bottom and side to side, overlapping strips along the way.

Add dimensional texture for a bunch of flower stickers (Frances Meyer) with torn and crumpled layers of colored tissue paper and tiny glass marbles.

3 Rub colored inkpads along torn edges; dip into embossing powder and heat. Slice into strips or design.

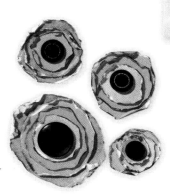

Torn, curled and layered flowers are a fresh and easy embellishment that can be made from a collection of scraps and a few buttons.

Image

Fractured Photos

No matter how hard we try, our photos don't always turn out like we'd like them to. But if we've captured a great moment, we want to scrap it anyway. This technique offers a creative way to feature a focal point, camouflage an unsightly background or add an unusual visual element to your layout.

A fractured photo is a photo that is sliced apart and then reassembled with some or all of its original pieces. Three styles of fractured photos are shown below.

All three styles require the selection of focal point(s). The number of focal points depends upon what is going on in your photo, i.e., the main area(s) of interest in your photo. I selected a few areas of interest in the seahorse photo, while the photo of my dog has only one focal point.

Supplies: *Repositionable adhesive; waxed paper; craft knife; ruler*

Tip Allow for extra space; the reassembled image will be larger than the original image because of the spaces in between the pieces!

VARIATIONS

Linear: Focal points that flow into a horizontal or vertical visual line are easy for the eye to follow, giving your design a clean, graphic look. A formal photo, such as the seahorse statue, works well with this type of fracture because of its simplicity.

❶ Begin with a large, simple image.

❷ Determine a focal point. I chose the seahorse head, the boy's head and torso, the boy's feet and the seahorse's tail. I added the belly of the seahorse to balance out the design. Draw a shape (square, circle, etc.) around desired focal point(s); keep the size of the shape relative to the area you're highlighting and relative to the size of the photo.

❸ Spray repositionable adhesive on the back of the photo; lay on wax paper. Cut out focal point segments using a craft knife and ruler. Reassemble segments one at a time onto a piece of cardstock or transparency, leaving space between each segment.

Shattered: A freehand-cut circle with radiating fragments brings the focal point of this photo right to the eyes of the dog. Using a ruler as a guide, place your craft knife at the edge of the circle and slice out toward the edge of the photo; continue around the circle as if you were slicing a pizza. Add interest to the design with a few horizontal and diagonal slices so your finished piece will look more like a shattered design rather than rays of sunshine.

Abstract: A class photo offers many potential points of interest to focus on. Layer selected focal points over a duplicate photo with foam spacers for added dimension.

Collage

Punched-Shape Collage

I was in the mood for a bit of extreme punch art one weekend that resulted in this detailed impressionistic collage of patterned papers. While it was a bit time-consuming, I found the process quite relaxing—no different from knit-one, purl-two a thousand times over! However, I am aware that the thought of such detail can make some scrapbookers turn the page faster than I can say "patterned paper!" I've simplified this technique so that you can do half the work and still achieve an artistic look.

Instead of covering the entire image with punched circles, you can achieve the look by fooling the eye with applied "dots" of color. Then you are free to top off the illusion with as many punched circles as you'd like.

Before you begin, select a simple landscape or still-life image. Copy or scan image to desired size; lighten image to about 30 percent and print two copies. Mark one copy "reference" and the other "design." You will be assembling the collage directly on top of the copy marked "design," so think of it as your paint-by-numbers guide!

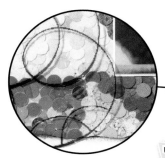

Supplies: Patterned papers (Club Scrap, Frances Meyer, Paper Adventures, Provo Craft); chalk palette or chalk inks; cotton swabs; adhesive; standard hole punch; tweezers

Tips Speed up the assembly of a detailed collage like this by choosing the right adhesive; I use a Xyron adhesive machine. The amount of time and effort you'll save with this tool is definitely worth the investment.

VARIATIONS

A collage of monochromatic punched squares (Creative Memories) emphasizes the graphic power of simplistic design.

1 Determine color values for the object(s) in your photo (see page 27 for how to do this). Select patterned papers accordingly. In my example:

    Sky = white to medium blue
    Sea = medium to dark blue
    Statue = patina greens and bronze
    Statue base = tan to brown

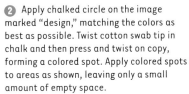

2 Apply chalked circle on the image marked "design," matching the colors as best as possible. Twist cotton swab tip in chalk and then press and twist on copy, forming a colored spot. Apply colored spots to areas as shown, leaving only a small amount of empty space.

Add an extra element of whimsy to patterned papers (Heidi Grace Designs) with a simple combination of punched shapes (Marvy/Uchida).

3 Fill empty areas by adhering circles punched from patterned papers. Use tweezers for quick and easy placement.

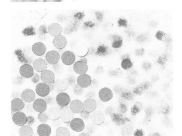

Slice and reassemble a bunch of wildflowers from punched and layered suns (Emagination Crafts, McGill).

Idea Notebook

Paper + Adhesive = Papier Colles

French words meaning "pasted papers"

The variety of papers to collage with is all around you; everything from junk mail to your daily newspaper can be used in a paper collage. If archival quality is a concern, treat found papers with an archival-preservation spray before using in a collage.

Types of papers to collage:

- *patterned*
- *stamped*
- *newspaper*
- *ephemera/maps*
- *textured*
- *dyed*
- *handmade*
- *wallpaper*

Enhance papers with:

Ephemera and found papers don't have to stay as you found them; change the color to match the tone or theme of your layout with your favorite colorant.

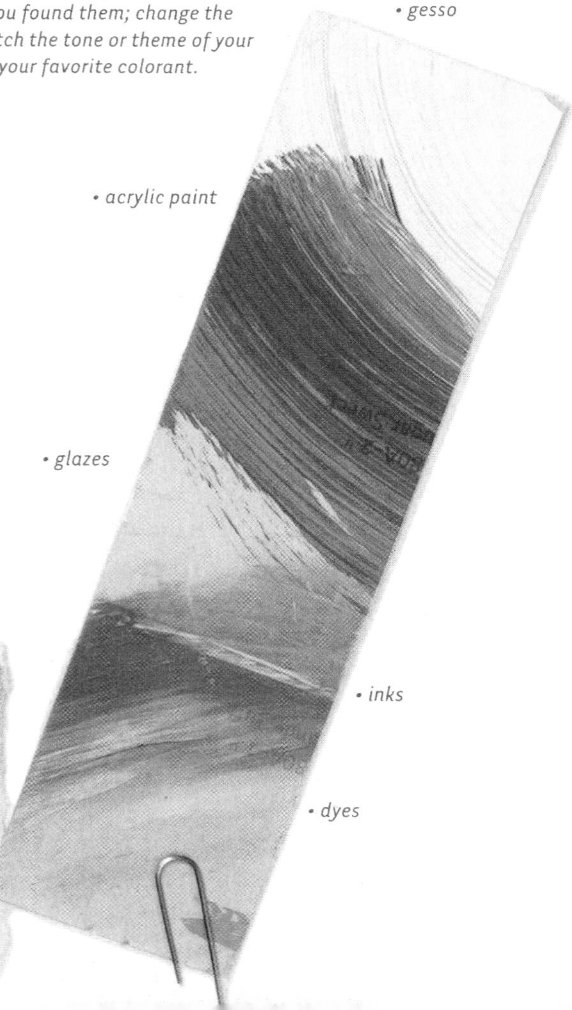

- *gesso*
- *acrylic paint*
- *glazes*
- *inks*
- *dyes*

Paper + Adhesive + Miscellaneous Elements = Dimensional Collage

The fun of collage starts before you even begin to cre-ate; it starts with the treasure hunt. Go through old jewelry boxes, junk drawers or even your kids' toy bins for fun and unique elements to integrate into your collage art. Dig into stored boxes of holiday treasures or heritage keepsakes for a meningful element. You'll be surprised at what you can find around your house to integrate into your collage.

Some elements to integrate:

- ribbon & fibers
- buttons, beads & sequins
- postage stamps
- ephemera, vintage items
- magazine images
- glitter
- charms & jewelry
- feathers
- pressed flowers & leaves

• assemblage

• magazine collage

• photo mosaic

The pop artists from the 60s and 70s were known for pushing the creative envelope when it came to looking at ordinary things in an extraordinary way. These artistic pioneers made bold personal and political statements about their post-war, iconic and consumer-driven society by fusing elements of art and images of real life together.

While assembling this inspiration board, I realized that the pop artists were not so different from us scrapbook artists are today in the way that we take the images from our very real lives and fuse them together with elements of art to create a look, style and statement that is all our own.

Get the Look

Pop Art

1 Take inspiration from a rainbow of bright colors and bold, curved shapes.

2 Integrate fabrics with fun, punchy circle patterns and coordinating stripes.

3 Catch the eye with a string of bold metallic accents.

4 Add Andy Warhol-style impact with repetitive images.

5 Look for new patterned paper designs that combine the geometric shapes in a pleasing palette of colors.

6 Turn one of your favorite photos into a pop culture with image-editing software. See www.macmerc.com/articles/Graphics_Tips/260 for instructions.

7 Integrate graphic flowers into your layouts; paper piece and layer a large flower or silhouette cut a single flower from patterned paper.

8 Make a strong design statement by pairing the simplicity of a black-and-white polka-dot or herringbone pattern with a shock of color.

9 You can never go wrong with clean striped lines of color; slice strips of solid-colored papers in varying widths or layer ribbon for extra texture.

10 Create art with words; collage a curved frame with colorful word stickers.

11 Today's saturated colors have lost a bit of the overdone pop art edginess. Maintain a sense of sophistication by surrounding colored elements with a good amount of white space.

12 Go with the flow; add curvy lines or designs with shaped rulers or templates and trim with scissors or a craft knife.

13 Look for inexpensive vintage jewelry at garage sales, flea markets or thrift stores for truly unique embellishments.

14 Pop artists integrated real-life elements that reflected the consumer-driven culture of the day. Look to the packaging of the products you use for inspirational designs.

15 Pop art meets paper art, resulting in a collage of patterned papers layered as a high-contrast image. The realistic collage technique on page 27 explains how to define color values.

16 Images created from gray or colored halftone dots are a signature look from the pop-art era. Replace enlarged colored halftone dots with enlarged colored pixels and you'll have a cool, contemporary design!

a l e x

Youth comes but once in a lifetime

- Henry Wadsworth Longfellow

1999

The Many Shades of Hue

Chapter 2

Have you ever found yourself strangely attracted to a design or an object but didn't know why? Chances are, you were attracted to its color because not only do we see color—we feel color. Studies show that our brain actually "sees" the color of an object before it identifies the object or gives words to our feelings. That's pretty powerful, and that is the power of color.

When it comes to picking colors to use in your layouts, take a chance with a color that speaks to you. Explore the association between the emotions you feel and the colors that come to mind; soon you will see how colors can easily take the place of your words.

Allow yourself to step aside from the "trendy" or "hot" colors of the moment and look to the memory you are scrapbooking. When you allow the power of color to be your expressive language, you allow it to reveal the many shades of hue.

Colorant

Tired of looking at leftovers? Don't throw them out...use them! Resurrect some of those leftover letter stickers you've got stashed away and use them as a mask to create a quick brayered design.

Texture

The ancient art of painting with wax, known as encaustic art, has found a new home within the world of collage. Smooth drops and scribblings from colorful beeswax crayons are melted into fascinating and vibrant textures.

Image

This technique took me back to the days when I used to doodle hearts, flowers and fancy letters on my notebook in school. I guess I never outgrew my desire to doodle, I just have gotten a few new tools to do it with!

Collage

34 photos, one layout—and my head isn't spinning when I look at it. What's my secret? Two design tools called scale and color value. You've heard it before; this is just a review and a new application...and a chance to lighten up a box of photos.

Layout supplies not listed with a technique can be found on page 122.

Essential Elements Diagram

Colorant	Texture	Image	Collage
Brayered Mask Effects	Colored Wax Scraffito	Photo Engraving	Multiphoto Mosaic

Colorant

Brayered Mask Effects

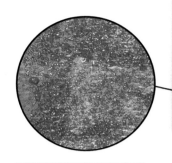

The faint illusion of ghosted letters adds a bit of mystery to a large silhouette-cut letter without taking away from the layout's design. This colorant technique is achieved in minutes using letter stickers as a mask and a brayer to apply the ink.

A mask is an item which is placed on a surface that prevents color from coming in contact with a specific area; think of it as the opposite of a stencil. In this technique, letter stickers are used as a mask, preventing the red ink from covering the entire surface and leaving a ghosted letter image.

Brayers are indispensable art tools because they allow you to roll on smooth applications of liquid color (paint, ink, etc.) in seconds. They are also used to smooth out air bubbles from collaged layers and secure lifted edges.

This technique has a ton of options...try using a different type of ink or textured cardstock, or assembling a mask of punched shapes or sticker designs.

Supplies: *Ancient Page dye re-inkers (Clearsnap); letter stickers (American Crafts, Creative Imaginations, Creative Memories, Doodlebug Designs, Making Memories, SEI, Sticker Studio); embossing powders (PSX Design, Stampendous!, Suze Weinberg); Versamark watermark ink pad (Tsukineko); brayer; waxed paper; tweezers*

VARIATIONS

A custom-made leaf mask, sliced from a transparency, is brayered with ColorBox chalk re-inkers (Clearsnap) as a unique background design.

1 Adhere letter stickers in one concentrated area of textured cardstock; mount the largest letters first and then fill with smaller letter stickers.

2 Drip two drops of each ink color on wax paper. Ink brayer by rolling back and forth over ink two to three times. Brayer inks over letter stickers back and forth both horizontally and vertically. Remove a few of the letter stickers with tweezers and re-adhere in another area of the cardstock. Repeat ink application and sticker relocation until the entire cardstock is covered with ink.

3 Let dry; remove all stickers. Rub watermark inkpad over inked collage; sprinkle with embossing powders and UTEE and heat with embossing gun. Silhouette cut into a large letter.

Create translucent layers by alternating pigment and dye inks (Clearsnap) on glossy cardstock. Heart stamp (EK Success); wings stamp (Mostly Animals).

Texture

Colored Wax Scraffito

Encaustic art is an ancient technique where colored waxes are melted, applied to a surface and then allowed to cool. Painting with wax results in amazing textures that just beg to be scratched, scraped or carved into, which is called *scraffito*. Objects, ephemera and scraps of paper can be embedded in warm wax, creating an illusionary sense of depth and mystery.

I have to admit that I do not work with wax in the ancient way; I'm too much of a modern girl! I like my wax colors nice and neat, already mixed together and packaged in a crayon or stick form. The crayons I use in this technique contain beeswax and are found in an art or craft store.

This technique is very basic but still very fun; it will give you an idea of what working with wax is like if you haven't done so before. Don't say I didn't warn you, though…once you play around with wax, you'll see how addicting it is!

Supplies: *Beeswax crayons (Inoxcrom); white paint pen (Sharpie); embossing heat gun or quilting iron; old paintbrush or cosmetic sponge; manicure stick*

Tips Regular crayons are a great way to experiment with a wax colorant technique, but they will produce different results. If you have a beeswax candle, melt a little beeswax with a heat gun and then add a few drops of a melted crayon for color. Blend the two together with a manicure stick or old paintbrush. Regular coloring crayons don't have enough actual wax in them to build up a texture.

VARIATIONS

This colorful abstract was made by layering one color of wax at a time onto crumpled and flattened paper. Black wax was applied last; splattered and smoothed into a swirl.

1 Color inside the lines of a printed number. Print number outline (or use a stencil) on white cardstock. Select two to three shades of a single color; scribble inside number with selected colors as shown.

2 Use an embossing gun or small quilting iron to melt the wax. Embossing gun: Heat the area until wax melts. Quilting iron: Place iron directly on the colored wax and smooth over cardstock; don't worry about going outside the lines, we'll take care of that in step 4. Let wax cool and then repeat steps 1 and 2 two more times.

3 Drip wax onto cardstock. Embossing gun: Hold the crayon over paper; teat tip with embossing gun. Dab melting tip onto paper five or six times. Heat wax with gun and spread with an old paintbrush or cosmetic sponge. Quilting iron: Press iron to tip of crayon; let wax drip (three to four drops is enough) onto cardstock. Smooth wax as described in step 1. You should now have a thick layer of wax; if not, repeat this step again.

4 Scratch into wax. Using a manicure stick or wooden skewer, scratch a diagonal crosshatch design in wax. Scrape wax from number outline; color with white paint pen and silhouette cut. If you're not happy with the scratched design, simply reheat and try again!

Colored wax was dripped onto an inkjet flower photo. After smoothing the wax, I used the edge and tip of the quilting iron to push the wax from the center of the flower out toward the edges, creating a soft ribbed texture.

Image
Photo Engraving

Scrapbooking doesn't always have to be about "the moments;" it can just be about "being." And sometimes we just have to be a little silly! My son takes such pride in being goofy (as most 7-year-olds do) that I decided to add a few comical and graphic elements to his photo—and yes, he begged me to doodle all over his face.

This kind of stylized doodling reminds me of all the hearts and flowers I used to draw in Geometry class when I didn't care about what others thought of my art. Things may be different now, but this type of freehand drawing leaves a lot of room for experimentation; there's no pressure to draw perfectly straight lines or sophisticated designs.

Sketch a few ideas on tracing paper with pencil before putting hot tool to photo. I highly suggest taking the time to practice and play with the heat tool on an extra photo or two. This technique works best on dark or colorful photos. Be sure to print photos on glossy photo paper for best results.

Supplies: *Transfer paper (Saral); Creative Hot Marks heat tool with stencil cutter point (Walnut Hollow); photo printed on glossy photo paper; pencil; vellum or tracing paper*

VARIATIONS

So quick and so fun! Add an Andy Warhol look to a bright and cheery daisy printed on glossy photo paper.

1 Place vellum or tracing paper over photo; trace outline of shirt and body onto tracing paper.

2 Layer tracing paper with designs over the photo. Place transfer paper between tracing paper and photo; trace over design with pencil. Lift tracing and transfer papers...voilà! Your design is ready to engrave.

3 Trace over design with Creative Hot Marks Tool. Keep the heat tool moving on the photo to prevent ugly brown marks or burn holes in your photo.

I love the look of an ornamental design on a black-and-white photo—especially when I can engrave it in minutes! A gold gel pen adds a touch of elegance to the engraved areas.

Collage

Multiphoto Mosaic

Now this is what I call organized chaos—34 photos assembled on one page! When it comes to creating a multiphoto layout, you've got to love the beauty of structured, linear rows; I know I do.

In order for a collage with this many images to keep from looking chaotic, I had to pay attention to the scale (size) and color value (shade) of the image. Both of these terms were introduced in Chapter I on pages 21 and 27 and are expanded upon here.

In regards to scale, I created two sets of each photo; one which featured my son's face very close up and the other, which had his face centered inside the square. The variation in head size allows the photos to have a uniform look without appearing the same.

When it came to color value, or tone of each photo, I separated the light-colored photos from the dark-colored photos so that one area of the collage would not consist of too many dark- (or light-) colored photos. Determining the difference between light- or dark-colored photos is easiest when the photos are next to one another (see example in step 2).

All in all, organizing a number of photos by scale and color value will help you assemble a visually balanced layout that is not chaotic.

Supplies: *Square punch (Creative Memories); white cardstock; craft knife; ruler; repositionable adhesive*

VARIATIONS

Landscape photos lend themselves to a layered multiphoto mosaic. Slice enlarged copies of an image into random segments. Alter segments with sandpaper or ink wash to create contrast. Layer and overlap to reassemble.

1 Crop photos into 1½" squares with a square punch or simply cut to size. Make a window-cropping tool to help you determine how your photos will look when cropped into a 1½" square; using a ruler and craft knife, slice a 1½" square in the middle of a cardstock scrap. Place window over photo as shown.

2 Separate photos into four piles according to color value and scale:
  1) light color value + close-up
  2) light color value + centered
  3) dark color value + close-up
  4) dark color value + centered

3 Alternate selection of light and dark photos as well as close-up and centered photos when placing photos in rows. Use a repositionable adhesive until you have determined placement of all photos. Select one photo from each pile and assemble in a row starting at the top of the page. This is not a hard and fast rule—simply a guideline to help you achieve a balanced layout when it comes to scale and color. Repeat until all rows are filled.

Colorant

Got grunge? No need to go out and buy it; you can have it any time you want after learning a simple paint technique called dry brushing. This technique is done as it sounds—by applying paint with a dry brush. Wait until you see how easy it is to create that edgy look you're yearning for.

Texture

Collage can't help but get a little more interesting when unusual textures and dimensional elements are incorporated into its layers. Look no further than the supplies you already have to turn a textile surface into a dimensional design.

Image

A printed or processed photo may be the end result to a photographer, but to me it is a canvas ready for experimentation. So when I came across an ink jet embossing cardstock that promised spectacular embossed effects, I had my doubts. Boy, was I in for a surprise!

Collage

Being a card-carrying member of the Instant-Gratification Generation, I often find myself making my own tools or supplies out of whatever I have on hand. On this occasion, I created a textured stamp based on a printing technique called a Collagraph to get the design I just couldn't live without!

Layout supplies not listed with a technique can be found on page 122.

Essential Elements Diagram

Colorant
Grunge Brushing
(background)

Texture
Dimensional
Stamping

Image
Embossed Photos

Collage
Collagraph
Prints

Colorant

Grunge Brushing

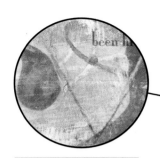

Do you love the edgy, acid-washed look that is seen on many popular patterned papers these days? The look you're seeing is a simulated dry brush paint technique that has been re-created digitally for printing. Learning how to dry brush is really quite easy because it is done just as it sounds. Painting with a dry brush keeps the bristles stiff so you can create that edgy look. Here are the two most important things to keep in mind when it comes to dry brushing:

• Remove excess paint from brush before applying on paper. After you dip the paintbrush into the paint, pounce the brush onto a paper towel a few times to remove the excess paint (so important!).

• Make certain that you allow each layer of paint to dry before applying the next so colors don't blend together.

Remember that it's only paint and paper; you're not going for neat and perfect—you're going for grunge!

Supplies: *Acrylic paint, matte medium (Golden); black cardstock; paper plate; large stiff paintbrush*

Tips The more layers of paint you apply, the longer the cardstock will take to dry! If you're going to paint, make good use of your time; pull out at least three or five pieces of cardstock and rotate the pieces while the others are drying.

VARIATIONS

A patriotic combination of colors looks dramatic when dry brushed on a black cardstock base.

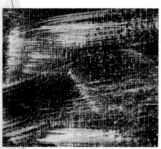

❶ Begin with the lightest color: in this case, white. Dip brush bristles into paint; firmly pounce brush on paper towels to remove excess paint. Brush white paint across cardstock with swift horizontal and vertical strokes. You are looking to add streaks of color, not coat the entire cardstock with paint. Let dry completely.

❷ Apply pink paint (a) in same manner as described above; let dry completely. Wipe brush off with paper towel (no water yet). As you apply brush strokes, keep in mind that you want to see some of the black cardstock background. Repeat paint technique with rose (b) and crimson (c) paint, making sure each layer dries before applying the next.

An unlikely color combination can work together with the dry brush technique if each layer is completely dry before applying the next. Violet, lavender, spring green, yellow green and white paints are layered over white cardstock background.

❸ At this point, I look at the painting and ask myself if the overall look is too dark, too light or just right. This piece was a little too dark, so I added a few more white and light pink brush strokes just as I applied the others.

Grunge goes glamorous! Blue glitter paint (Stewart Gill) adds a touch of glam to the striking combination of black, white, lime green and turquoise.

Turn to page 65 to see how dry brushing can completely transform patterned paper!

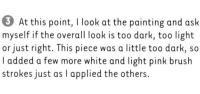

technique Texture
Dimensional Stamping

There's no reason why your stamped images need to remain flat; give your stamps a new look by taking them to a higher dimension!

A simple cut-and-reassemble technique transforms an embossed velvet rose into an elegant and dimensional embellishment. Try this technique with one of your own foam stamps, a different type of fabric or a cool textured or handmade paper. Instead of embossing the image with an iron, stamp the image with watermark ink and emboss with clear UTEE and a heat gun. Select a bold stamp design with deeply carved lines for easier cutting and reassembly.

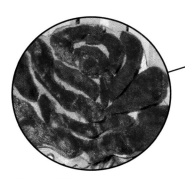

Supplies: *Foam stamp (Plaid); Versamark watermark inkpad (Tsukineko); clear embossing powder (Stamp n' Stuff); ColorBox red chalk inkpad (Clearsnap); water in spritzer bottle; velvet fabric; iron; silver metallic cardstock; small, sharp scissors; foam adhesive; silk leaves*

1 Place velvet plush-side down on rubber stamp. Lightly spritz with water before pressing hot iron firmly on stamp for 15-20 seconds. Do not move iron from side to side; lift iron and velvet to see embossed image.

2 Stamp flower with watermark ink on silver cardstock; lightly sprinkle with clear embossing powder and set with heat gun. This will serve as a placement guide for re-assembling cut flower sections. I've stamped the flower in the photo with white ink so that you can see it.

3 Using small, sharp scissors, cut velvet flower sections apart along embossed lines. Reassemble each section right after cutting with foam spacers onto stamped cardstock as shown. After reassembling entire flower, silhouette cut leaving about a 1/16" border. Mount with painted silk leaves.

VARIATIONS

Shape stamped sea treasures (Just for Fun Rubber Stamps) into unique three-dimensional art. Color images stamped on shrink plastic with alcohol inks (Ranger). Heat with embossing gun; carefully shape and meld plastic pieces together while warm.

A silhouette-cut, stamped art-deco design transforms into a dimensionally elegant embellishment when layered over patterned paper with foam spacers.

Image

Embossed Photos

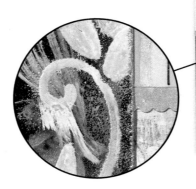

I'm always looking for ways to add unique effects to photographs, so I thought I'd try my hand at embossing a few. After creating a lot of, shall we say, unsightly textures (blisters), I found an ink jet embossing cardstock that keeps the ink wet long enough to sprinkle and set embossing powder. It sounded too good to be true, and I had my doubts about the results.

I experimented with clear, colored and glittered powders and a number of printed photos and designs—and the results were beautiful! I never would have thought that I could create such gorgeous effects with an inkjet printer. You will be amazed at what you can do with this paper, a little bit of embossing powder and your wonderfully creative mind.

Supplies: *Embossing paper (Imagination Gallery); clear embossing powder (Stamp'n Stuff); decorative stencil (Plaid); Versamark watermark pen (Tsukineko); metallic rub-ons (Robin Inc.); verdigris embossing powder (Clearsnap); white embossing powder; baby wipes; fixative spray (Prismacolor)*

Tip Remove stray embossing powder with a thin paintbrush before setting with heat.

1 Sprinkle clear embossing powder immediately over just-printed photo; shake off loose powder and heat with embossing gun. Set aside for about 10 minutes. Grab a baby wipe; lightly rub over photo, except for the face area. Any ink that isn't covered with embossing powder will come off, creating a soft, dreamy effect.

2 Place stencil over right side of photo; trace design with watermark pen. Sprinkle white embossing powder over design; set with heat.

3 Apply silver and pink metallic rub-ons over design with fingers. Rub watermark inkpad along photo edges; dip into verdigris embossing powder and set with heat.

VARIATIONS

Have you ever noticed how the ocean sparkles when the sun hits it? Create a similarly dazzling effect with a mix of rainbow glitter embossing powder (Stampendous!), sapphire pearluster (Stampendous!) and pearl UTEE (Suze Weinberg).

Surround a photo subject with positive words and encouraging phrases (Stampa Rosa); mask face with a post-it note. Silver embossing powder (PSX Design); platinium UTEE (Suze Weinberg).

Collage

Collagraph Prints

I don't mind making things when I need to since I am an instant-gratification kind of girl. I was already in the middle of this project when I realized I would never find a stamp large enough to create the design I visualized in my head, so I set out to make my own stamp based on a printing technique called a *collagraph*.

A collagraph is a form of printing collaged materials that are mounted on a stiff backing called a "plate." While this collagraph only consists of hemp string and cardboard, a number of textured items can be adhered to a plate before it is inked and pressed for an image. Try assembling buttons, leaves, molding paste or glue swirls for an interesting printed design. You'll not only have a one-of-a-kind design, you'll also have a new stamp that can be used again and again. This is a "perfectly imperfect" technique, which means that the printed design will most likely have a grungy look to it rather than perfectly straight and evenly inked lines.

Supplies: *Quick-dry liquid adhesive (Duncan); gesso, acrylic paint (Golden); cardboard; pencil; ruler; hemp string; paintbrush*

VARIATIONS

Make a collagraph plate in minutes with precut, self-adhesive foam shapes (Fibre Craft) adhered to a cardboard plate.

1 Cut cardboard to desired size; draw diagonal lines using a pencil and ruler. Cut hemp string about 2" longer than drawn lines. Apply quick-drying glue along pencil lines; press hemp string into glue and hold until set.

plate

resulting design

2 Brush on a coat of gesso before applying ink or paint to prevent the color from soaking into the cardboard plate (this is optional but suggested!). Brush black paint or ink on collagraph plate.

A collage of found textured elements (acrylic slides, metal stars, bubble wrap, buttons and plastic tubing) make for a unique printing plate and printed design.

plate

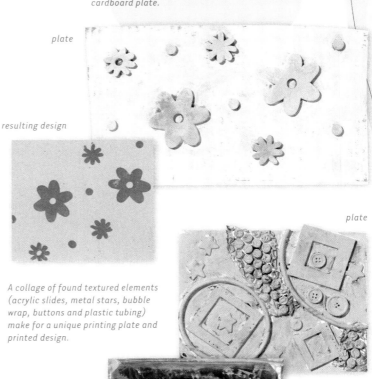

3 Place the plate facedown on cardstock to print relief design. Press firmly with both hands; carefully lift off. Wipe plate off with a baby wipe after print is made.

resulting design

 Tips Work quickly as acrylic paint and inks dry fast. You can add a small amount of matte medium to acrylic paint to slow drying time.

Colorant

The thought of painting paper can be quite daunting; it's so permanent, and what happens if you make a mistake? Well, I say this: It's only paper! Once you see how easy it is to alter the look of any patterned paper or cardstock, you'll never be without the perfect colored paper again!

Texture

If you're thinking the embellished accents on this page look like they were crafted from a soda can, you're right! Aluminum's thin and malleable surface is easy to cut, bend, shape and form into unique, rustic or even delicate accents.

Image

In my world, no surface is safe from experimentation or alteration. The unusual pairing of paint and plastic adds a whole new atmosphere to printed transparent images.

Collage

What do you do when a great technique has gone wrong? Take a deep breath and dig deep for creative inspiration! After a bit of thinking, I came up with a way to turn a failed photo transfer into a winning technique!

Layout supplies not listed with a technique can be found on page 122.

Youth comes but once in a lifetime
Henry Wadsworth Longfellow

Colorant
Altered
Patterned Paper

Texture
Aluminum
Accents

Image
Painted
Transparencies

Collage
Layered
Photomontage

Colorant

Altered Patterned Paper

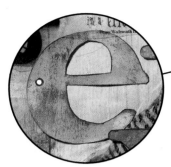

How many times have you looked through your stockpile of patterned papers only to realize you don't have something in the color you need? What if you could change the color of any patterned paper in a matter of minutes?

This technique is as easy as applying a coat of acrylic paint onto a patterned paper and then quickly wiping across the painted surface with a baby wipe. Wiping the paint off with in this manner allows the paper's pattern to show through a stain of color. The secret to applying a quick and smooth coat of paint is to use a brayer instead of a paintbrush.

Supplies: *Patterned paper (Design Originals); acrylic paints (Golden); Mica Magic inkpads (Clearsnap); green paper; baby wipes; letter and design stamps (antique printer's stamps)*

❶ Mix paint with matte medium. Brayer paint over patterned paper; quickly wipe across painted surface with a baby wipe and let dry.

❷ Lighten paint color by mixing remaining paint with a small amount of white paint. Brayer paint and wipe surface with a baby wipe. Lightly spritz surface with alcohol and blot with paper towel to remove more paint; repeat until desired clarity of patterned paper is achieved.

❸ Stamp designs and letters with green, charcoal and beige inks. Rub across painted paper with black inkpad.

VARIATIONS

Transform your patterned paper from this...to this!

before

after

before

after

Blend different colored patterned papers together with a quick wash of paint. First brayer ivory paint over layered patterned papers; quickly wipe surface with a baby wipe to blend.

before

after

Texture

Aluminum Accents

When I'm on a hunt for new ideas, anything and everything I come across has creative possibility. So imagine the look on my husband's face when I poured out the remainder of his soda and began cutting into the can! Well, that can turned into part of the dimensional flower art on the cover of this book, which in turn inspired the embellishments and accents on this page.

Aluminum cans or metal foils found in craft stores are wonderfully malleable. Their lightweight texture allows them to be cut, bent, shaped and formed into unique decorative elements. Alter the surface with permanent inkpads, alcohol inks, acrylic paint, sandpaper and even rub-on designs. Look for items at the grocery store that come in decorative tins and take advantage of some really unique and colorful designs.

Pair aluminum shapes with toolbox findings, dress it up with colored wire and beads, or soften the look with fabric or fiber ties. However you dress up aluminum art, you'll be turning the ordinary into extraordinary!

Supplies: *Decorative rub-ons (Li'l Davis Designs); Staz-On permanent/solvent ink (Tsukineko); soda can; utility scissors or tin snips; sandpaper; decorative scissors*

Tip Use caution when cutting into an aluminum can; unfinished edges are very sharp! Remove can top with ease by placing scissors into drink opening; snip and then turn can horizontal. Start cutting around can at snipped area.

VARIATIONS

Fold a freeform frame around a mini collage glazed with crystal lacquer.

❶ Very carefully, cut top and bottom from soda can with heavy scissors; trim off jagged or sharp edges. Next, cut down can's seam to open. Bend aluminum opposite its natural curve; flatten under heavy books if necessary.

❷ Distress front and back of aluminum with sandpaper; rub permanent inkpad over aluminum.

Grow a garden of whimsical bottle cap flowers (Li'l Davis Designs). Flatten with hammer; attach eyelet. Color with Adirondack alcohol inks (Ranger) and add microbeads. Fashion stem and leaf from aluminum strips and wire.

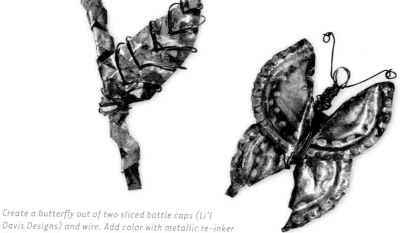

❸ Cut and shape aluminum as desired: trim with decorative scissors, bend, fold, punch, etc. Apply rub-on design for tag. Attach to page with eyelets.

Create a butterfly out of two sliced bottle caps (Li'l Davis Designs) and wire. Add color with metallic re-inker (Clearsnap) and Adirondack alcohol inks (Ranger).

Image
Painted Transparencies

In my world, no surface is safe from experimentation. This also seems to be evident in the scrapbook world, where we have seen the possibilities of surface exploration reach heights we never dreamed possible. And with images showing up on everyday items, textiles and common office products, the allure of adding a colored signature to whatever captures my fancy is certainly more than I can resist.

Stippled strokes of acrylic paints and inks applied to the back of a printed transparency transform the atmosphere of an image in minutes. Since painting behind an image is a little out of the ordinary, there are a few things to keep in mind:

- Apply colors lightly at first; a little goes a long way.
- Pounce loaded brush on scrap paper to remove most of the colorant before applying to transparency.
- Clean up stray ink before it dries with cotton swabs.
- Check your progress; turn the transparency over to see the effects you've added.

Print or copy an image of a person and follow along with the steps below. Keep in mind acrylic paint produces a more opaque effect behind a transparency than ink does.

Supplies: *ColorBox chalk and pigment inks (Clearsnap); fixative spray (Prismacolor); printed transparency; stippling brush or small stiff paintbrush; cotton swabs; baby wipes*

Tips When working with paints and inks, use a sticky-note as a mask to protect an area from receiving color. Lighten an inked/painted area by stippling with a clean brush to remove some of the ink/paint.

VARIATIONS

Aquacolor crayons, a touch of water and metallic paint pen breathes life into a printed black-and-white sunflower.

before

after

Acrylic paint adds playful spirit to a text-printed transparency (Creative Imaginations).

1 Turn transparency to wrong side. Tap a small, stiff paintbrush into paint/ink; pounce brush on scrap paper to remove most of the color before applying on transparency. Stipple light colors before adding dark colors. Wipe color from brush with a dry paper towel and stipple again to blend. For a touch of vintage, add a few taps of copper ink in select areas.

2 Add color to face. Skin colors can be tricky, so experiment on a scrap piece of paper. I blended Yellow Ochre, Copper and Rousillon (brick red) for the skin color (in order). Wipe color from brush with a dry paper towel and stipple again to blend. Spray with fixative spray when finished.

Metallic re-inkers (Clearsnap) and a metallic paint pen illuminate the murky waters of the bayou.

Collage

Layered Photomontage

I have to be honest and admit that this technique resulted from a resurrected "flopportunity." I was having one of those days when nothing turned out as planned, including an image transfer I was working on. How was I ever going to salvage a newly painted background with a bad image transfer? After hours of frustration, my desperation somehow turned into inspiration: I decided to layer it.

I used this technique twice on this layout. I layered the focal point photo as well as the background illustration of the boys. The photo is a layering of a torn photo segment over a painted transparency. The illustration is a layering of a segment of a painted transparency over an image transfer (see page 108 for transfer technique). The concept is so simple, but one I had not considered before having to search for a solution.

Moral of the story: Remember to pull from your own inventive and resourceful mind; you've got all the answers you need!

Supplies: *Transparency*

Tip Dry brush paint over layered image to create a subtle yet consistent look to the layered element.

Layered Photomontage
Photo + Painted Transparency = Layered Image

VARIATIONS

Show age progression with sliced and layered portrait photos. Reduce or enlarge one photo to desired size; measure one element that is consistent in photo (top to bottom of face). Reduce or enlarge remaining photos so selected element is same size in each photo.

} Idea Notebook

Photopainting: Add an artistic element to your photos with your favorite colorant.

Colored Pencils (left center)

Give the illusion of art on canvas; print photo on linen textured cardstock. Blend colors together by coloring over with white pencil. Color lightest areas first and then darken as desired.

Color Wash & Outline (left bottom)

Spray inkjet photos with sealant (Prismacolor) before applying liquid colorant (so ink colors don't bleed with paint). Add water to a small amount of acrylic paint to create a watercolor wash. Draw loose outline with a Sharpie.

Acrylic Paint (below)

Wipe over photo painted with acrylic glaze to remove excess and achieve an uneven appearance. Lightly dampen along edges of photo and scratch with fingernail to achieve distressed border.

Edgy Patterned Papers

Use the Grunge Brush paint technique on page 54, along with a few of the ideas below, to add an edgy look to any patterned paper.

• Create scratchy and smudged lines and circles: Draw thin lines using white or black fine line paint pens and a ruler; trace jar lids for circles. Quickly smudge ink/paint with finger tip along drawn line.

• Ghosted graphics: Stamp images with white ink; lightly blot stamped design with tissue while wet to remove some of the ink.

• Paint splotches: Shake paint pen; press down with tip on scrap paper to get paint to flow. Hold over patterned paper and quickly flick tip toward patterned paper.

• Grungy letters/text: Apply two or three sizes of letter stamps overlapping another with white, black, gray or brown inks; blot with tissue while wet or rub with sandpaper after ink dries.

• Remove paint in areas: Wipe away damp paint with a baby wipe. Remove dried paint by spritzing with alcohol and then wiping with a baby wipe.

Get the Look

Faux Screenprint Designs

1 Assemble punched shapes: Create a faux screen-print pattern with basic punched shapes in bold and fresh colors.

2 Stamp designs in monochromatic colors: Bold decorative foam stamps are perfect for creating a screen-printed tone-on-tone background. Ink a foam stamp with a brayer for an evenly inked design or haphazardly apply ink to a stamp for the look of a worn screen-print design.

3 Stencil technique: A decorative stencil is one of the easiest ways to create the look of a screen-print (see page 122 for instructions).

4 Sticker mask technique: If this look isn't fab, I don't know what is...and it's so easy to do using letter stickers as a mask (see page 122 for directions).

5 Layer a decorative dingbat font: The Internet has a ton of free font sites; look for a decorative or themed dingbat font like the leaf font used here. Enlarge to desired size and apply monochromatic colors. Print, silhouette cut and layer.

6 Freehand draw and cut contemporary geometric pattern: Uneven lines and rounded corners add charm and urban appeal to this design. Look to fashion and home magazines for a modern mix of colors.

7 Use clip-art resources: Take advantage of online clip-art resources for line art images and designs that make creating the look of a screen-print super easy.

8 Trace magazine images: You say you're not an illustrator? No worries! Magazines such as Outdoor Life and National Geographic are full of beautifully photographed images of flora and fauna that can be traced to create stunning silhouettes (see page 122 for directions).

9 Trace body outlines: Look to your photos for realistic and expressive body shapes. Trace outline with tracing paper; copy or scan and print onto patterned or colored paper. Add details and outline with white pen.

The return of all things 60s and 70s has catapulted contemporary, screen-printed designs into everything from fashion to home décor. Pop artist Andy Warhol made the unique, graphic look of screen-printed designs popular. The simplicity of the shaped silhouettes and flat colors (color without shading or dimension) makes these designs easy to duplicate with scrapbook and art supplies. Try a few of the techniques I've come up with to create your own faux screen-printed designs; look to fashion and home décor magazines for contemporary color combinations and design inspiration.

Where did the Time Go?

3 Under the Surface

What drives you to create your layouts? Are you driven to get in touch with your personal history and sense of self by documenting your feelings about what is special and meaningful in your life? Or are you motivated to work and create with your hands, transforming and manipulating the simplest of materials into beautiful and unique layouts?

Neither is right or wrong, but both define the texture of your scrapbook pages. By definition, texture refers to the quality or "feel" of a surface. Whether we are talking about the surface of ourselves—what we are made of—or the surface of our layouts, texture plays an important role in communicating the depth of our personal experiences.

Texture is more than what's on the surface. It weaves structure and character into our compositions, changing the way they look and feel to reflect our inner voice.

Colorant

Don't let the word "crayon" fool you; watercolor crayons are a versatile coloring tool that can be used dry or blended with a wet paintbrush. Imagine getting the look of a vibrant watercolor wash without the fear of painting!

Texture

Discover a new kind of canvas for scrapbook art; the smooth and sturdy surface of foam core welcomes a number of artistic techniques making it the perfect foundation for unique and decorative effects.

Image

How do you satisfy your urge to embellish? Whether you like a little or a lot, you'll love enhancing images with techniques that combine the tradition of surface design with the creativity of art.

Collage

The new look of decoupage takes inspiration from bold botanical prints, shabby-chic florals, quaint architectural designs and even graphic geometric prints—layered together in unexpected combinations for surprising results.

Layout supplies not listed with a technique can be found on page 122.

Colorant	Texture	Image	Collage
Watercolor Washes	Textured Foam Core	Embellished Fabric	Dimensional Decoupage

technique

Colorant

Watercolor Washes

Imagine being able to create gorgeous painterly effects without having to learn traditional watercolor technique. Working with watercolor crayons (also known as aquacolor crayons) will exceed your colorant expectations, especially when it comes to versatility and results.

Practice layering scribbled colors next to and on top of each other; blend on cardstock with a wet paintbrush instead of a palette like traditional paints.

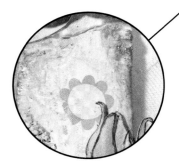

Tip Note how the color becomes vibrant and blends easily. Keep blended colors beautiful; clean your brush often!

Supplies: *Watercolor crayons (Lyra); paintbrush; water; paper towels*

Foam core + patterned paper + watercolor crayon = foam core frame.

VARIATIONS

❶ Select three shades of one color; scribble on watercolor paper or cardstock as shown, making sure to leave some white space on paper. Add a little bit of color at first; you can always add more.

The versatility of watercolor crayons is evident when used to create a stamped watercolor design. Scribble crayons directly onto the rubber stamp (Anna Griffin); lightly spritz with water and then stamp.

❷ Dip medium-sized paintbrush into water; dab excess on paper towel. Move brush over light colors two to three times with loose strokes.

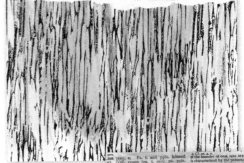

Textured cardstock (Club Scrap) is infused with a wash of color in seconds.

❸ Move light-colored wash into dark color; brush over a few times until there is no clearly defined lines between light and dark, blending colors into one another. When brush feels dry, dip in water again; blot off on paper towel and brush over colors. Repeat until all colors are blended.

A wash of vibrant color can completely change the look of patterned text paper (7 Gypsies).

Texture

Textured Foam Core

Hours of reckless experimentation has led me down many roads; some I'd rather not travel again, yet others I find myself eager to revisit. One of my many journeys left me looking at foam core as a new kind of canvas for scrapbook art.

Foam core is a lightweight yet sturdy material that comes in a variety of thicknesses. Its smooth surface welcomes a number of artistic techniques which makes it a perfect foundation for unique and decorative effects; it can be textured and distressed, collaged and painted, incised or etched.

Whether you cut it into a tag, photo mat or frame, elevate layers of elements, or carve out a niche for found objects, we have only scratched the surface of foam core's creative possibilities.

Supplies: *Versamark watermark inkpad or pen (Tsukineko); gold and clear UTEE (Suze Weinberg); craft knife; heat gun*

Tip Melted plastic foam has an odor; heat in a ventilated area. Keep moving the embossing gun; intense heat can turn plastic foam brown quickly.

VARIATIONS

Display school supplies and memorabilia in sliced foam core windows.

Make a dimensional statement with an over-sized decorative parenthesis. Use a hot craft knife tool to slice through the foam core in seconds.

1 Remove foam core "skin." Using a craft knife, slice into the outer layer with diagonal strokes; do not press knife all the way through foam core. Peel off the foam core's outer layer. Slice again into exposed areas of plastic foam to roughen up the texture.

2 Emboss exposed areas. Press Versamark pad or color with watermark pen onto exposed plastic foam areas. Sprinkle clear and gold UTEEs; heat with an embossing gun.

Treasures from the sea rest inside a carved photo niche.

It's time to get personal because personalizing is hot right now! In the scrapbook world, the happy cohabitation of photos, fabric and paper has created an explosion of embellishments that call out to our decorative egos. Adding your own style and accents to any kind of surface including textile images and designs is what it's all about.

Enhance a scrap of fabric with beaded details or frame a printed image with fibers. Whatever elements you choose to embellish with, personalizing the surfaces of a printed image has never been so much fun.

Supplies: *Cotton fabric sheet for inkjet printer (Jacquard Products); watercolor pencils (Staedtler); patterned fabric; fusible web; iron; water; paintbrush; fibers; pearl beads; sewing needle and thread*

VARIATIONS

Create a feminine photo frame with a unique combination of silk, metal and burlap. Copy patterned paper and photo onto silk paper sheet (Jacquard Products); adhere iron-on metal studs (Cousin Corp.) around photo. Enhance burlap with watercolor crayon wash before layering under silk printed photo.

1 Print image on cotton fabric sheet. Color areas with watercolor pencils using light diagonal strokes. Color face and skin with desired skin-tone pencils using very light strokes. Blend by coloring over with white pencil; do not blend with water!

2 Dip a small paintbrush in water; dab on paper towel before applying on colored areas. Lightly brush over penciled color, blending pencil lines. The water will make colored areas look darker; however, as fabric dries, colored areas will lighten back up.

3 Stitch twisted fibers along edge of fabric page. String pearls and dangle from button sewn at upper left corner.

A fancy toile pattern becomes a contemporary design with the addition of sequins, beads and glitter glue.

Collage
Dimensional Decoupage

Decoupage, also known as paper sculpting or paper tole, is experiencing a contemporary revival due to the rising popularity of paper arts. This simple decorative technique consists of cutting, shaping and mounting images onto a plain or painted surface.

The new look of decoupage takes inspiration from bold botanical prints, shabby-chic florals, quaint architectural designs and colorful geometric patterns. Images can be decoupaged singly or as dimensionally layered designs using foam spacers or silicone glue. Mount silhouette-cropped images onto unusual or faux-painted surfaces for a stylish and artistic design.

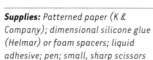

Supplies: *Patterned paper (K & Company); dimensional silicone glue (Helmar) or foam spacers; liquid adhesive; pen; small, sharp scissors*

VARIATIONS

Tissue paper and creatively cut and layered designs give the illusion of a dimensional flower blooming from a concrete surface.

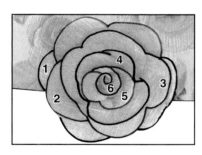

1 Make seven copies of image on printed paper (page 121); six to cut and one for reference. Before cutting, define areas of image that can be separated and layered; mark on reference copy as shown.

An artful witch hides her frightful smile behind layers of dimensionally lacquered features.

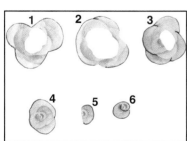

2 Silhouette-crop layers as defined, one from each copy. Write layer numbers on back of cut pieces for easy reassembly.

3 Reassemble the image starting with layer 1. Mount layer 1 with liquid adhesive onto cardstock. Mount layers 2 through 6 with dimensional silicone glue or foam spacers. Look at reference copy for reassembly guidance.

A stunning title page is skillfully cut and layered from elegant patterned paper.

Colorant

Can you resist a little bit of excitement? Take a look at how techniques such as masks and resists build anticipation and add an element of surprise to the creative process.

Texture

Decorative embellishments, like a fabulous purse, can pull a look together and make your layout shine. Add a little something special to the surface of your pages and you'll see how easy it is to go from ordinary to extraordinary!

Image

The fascinating world of image transfers opens up a whole new avenue of creative possibilities. If you haven't been persuaded to try one yet, this is the technique that may change your mind; it's easy, it's quick and its results are amazing!

Collage

Assembling a dimensional collage is like embarking on an expedition into the unknown. Through experimentation, items like ephemera, found objects and colorants are transformed into a single artistic element.

Layout supplies not listed with a technique can be found on page 123.

Time *in a* bottle...

Ten Year Anniversary...April 10. 2003
The Venetian Hotel. Las Vegas
who would have thought that one fateful day in the paper aisle of Office Depot would lead to a decade of love and the birth of a beautiful family. And while we may be ten years older in age, ten years wiser in life, and ten years longer in love, I want you to know that forever doesn't describe how long you will be "The One"

You're the one true thing I know I can believe in... I love you

Colorant
Reverse
Stencil Mask

Texture
Encrusted
Embellishments

Image
Decal Image
Transfer

Collage
Dimensional
Collage

Colorant

Reverse Stencil Mask

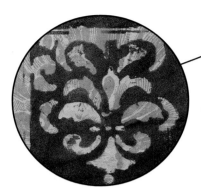

I think one of the reasons scrapbooking is such an addictive hobby is due in part to the element of surprise. The blank page presents itself as a new possibility…a creative surprise we give to ourselves every time we begin to create.

I am reminded about the element of surprise whenever I incorporate a mask or resist technique into my art. Masks and resists prevent color from coming in contact with a specific area with materials such as wax, tape, rubber cement, masking fluid, paper or embossing powder. This technique explores the use of masking tape and a masking fluid as the resist.

Supplies: *Patterned paper (C-Thru Ruler); removable artist's tape (3M); repositional adhesive spray (Delta); decorative stencil (Plaid); masque pen (Cruddas Innovations) or rubber cement; acrylic paints (Golden); small foam brush; brayer*

VARIATIONS

Create an air of mystery amongst an elegant layering of stamped designs with an embossed resist of watermark ink and brayered dye that resisted a stenciled feather mask. Feather stamp (Rubber Stampede); face stamp (Just for Fun Rubber Stamps); feather stencil (Stewart Gill); polka dots (Hero Arts); Versamark watermark ink pad (Tsukineko); dye ink (Clearsnap); clear embossing powder (Stampendous!)

① Adhere torn and sliced tape frame on patterned paper as shown; press edges down firmly. Notice that tape strips are not cut or sliced perfect. Spray repositionable adhesive on back of stencil; position on patterned paper. Apply a thin coat of liquid mask with foam brush. Remove stencil before mask dries.

② After mask dries, brayer acrylic paint over masked design; set design aside to dry.

③ Now for the fun part! Rub the liquid mask with fingertips to reveal design. Carefully peel off the masking tape and discard.

Design yourself a quick-and-easy monogram. Paint a rubber cement resist on glossy cardstock before sponging on a warm mix of dye inks (Clearsnap).

Texture

Encrusted Embellishments

Nothing compares to the fun of adding a fabulous finishing touch to your layout. Raise the surface of your embellishments by encrusting them with shiny and sparkly elements.

Encrusting is a fancy term for covering or coating a surface with an element. Whether you assemble a collection of jewels, beads, sequins, mosaic tiles, shells, mirror squares, glass shards, tiny glass marbles, coins or buttons, you're sure to create a unique and personalized embellishment. Look for surfaces that can hold decorative elements like molding paste, gel medium, melted wax, UTEE, resin, clay, hot glue, thick paint. Be creative and have fun turning the ordinary into extraordinary!

Supplies: *Versamark watermark ink pad (Tsukineko); gold UTEE (Suze Weinberg); heavy cardstock; scissors; aluminum foil; heat gun; double-stick tape; tweezers; seashells; pearl beads; manicure stick*

VARIATIONS

Snippets of photo scraps set in regular gel medium take on a stylish shine.

Bring on the bling with layers of sparkling sequins (Gutermann).

Encrust a mix of mosaic jewels and glass beads in molding paste for a fresh change.

Enhance a painted slide mount with dried flowers encrusted in dimensional paint (Texture Magic, Delta).

The unique style of a glass and jeweled texture (Stewart Gill) becomes even more striking when set in black UTEE.

1 Cut heart from heavy cardstock; mount with double-stick tape onto aluminum foil. Press watermark inkpad onto heart; sprinkle with gold UTEE and set with heat. Repeat four to five times, creating a thick foundation.

2 Reheat UTEE until soft; pull heat away and drop largest shells into melted UTEE with tweezers. Quickly sprinkle a small amount of UTEE powder over placed shells and reheat from underneath heart so UTEE crystals don't fly around. Press shells into warm UTEE to secure.

3 Heat UTEE until soft; place small shells and pearls, moving elements around in hot UTEE with a manicure stick. Sprinkle lightly with UTEE and heat from underneath as described above. Repeat until heart is covered. Press watermark pad over encrusted shape and sprinkle with clear UTEE; set with heat.

Image

Decal Image Transfer

The fascinating world of image transfers (transferring an image from one surface to another) is nothing short of magical. While there are a number of image transfer techniques that you can do, I get better results using a product called Lazertran.

Lazertran is a decal paper that can be used with inkjet printers or color copiers, which means that any image that can be printed or copied can be transferred onto another surface (please respect copyright laws!). The image can then be painted or glazed with decorative brush strokes. I really like that Lazertran picks up the texture of the surface it's mounted on while retaining amazing photo clarity.

Supplies: *Acrylic gloss medium, acrylic gel medium, acrylic pearl paint (Golden); Lazertran decal paper; bowl of water; textured cardstock or watercolor paper; foam brush; fan paintbrush; baby wipes*

? Why would you want to transfer a photo? My answer is this: creative possibilities. Having the option to take an image off of the page and place it on another surface, i.e., a tag, microscope slide, piece of fabric or photo album cover, opens up a whole new world of creative possibilities.

VARIATIONS

1 Copy or print photo on Lazertran decal paper; trim image to size. Soak decal in water according to manufacturer's instructions (different for inkjet and color copier). Decal will curl in water; this is normal. Remove image from water; place facedown on paper towel. Slide backing off from decal. Gently blot and set aside to dry.

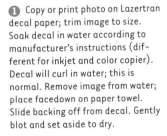

2 Brush a thin layer of gloss medium on cardstock with foam brush. Place decal transfer on wet medium face up. Dab fingertips in gloss medium before rubbing out bubbles to prevent decal from tearing. Gently smooth out decal with fingers, removing air bubbles as you smooth. Let dry.

Create a unique urban image by slicing a design into an image transfer of a map layered over a photograph.

3 Create textured lines with a fan paintbrush and clear soft gel medium. Brush a thin coat of gel medium over image with one-way vertical strokes; let dry. Repeat with horizontal and diagonal strokes, allowing gel medium to dry in between each application. Complete the look with a thin coat of pearlescent paint; paint on and wipe across surface with a baby wipe, removing some of the wet paint.

Decorative swirls add to the ambiance of a romantic photo. Stamp design on decal transfer sheet before mounting over photograph.

Collage

Dimensional Collage

Are you feeling adventurous? Assembling a dimensional collage is like embarking on an expedition into the unknown; the search for a collection of items begins with nothing more than a thought or inspiration. Through experimentation, items such as ephemera and found objects are layered amongst mixed media techniques, transforming combinations of color, texture and shape into a single artistic element.

Look to the theme of your layout for inspiration, and then look at the supplies you have and think of new ways to use them. When it came to creating the bottle in the sand, I stamped the image on a piece of clear shrink plastic with no intention of shrinking it, and I mixed tiny glass marbles into the molding paste to add texture to the sand.

Remember, even if you're not sure about where you're going with your dimensional collage, you can always enjoy the ride!

Supplies: *Acrylic gloss medium (Golden) or PVA; clear shrink plastic (Lucky Squirrel); vintage bottle stamp (Just for Fun Rubber Stamps); permanent black solvent ink pad (Tsukineko); alcohol inks (Ranger); molding paste, acrylic paints (Golden); map ephemera; blue vellum; foam brush; small paintbrush; alcohol in spritzer bottle; tiny glass marbles; palette knife; liquid adhesive; tweezers; patterned paper; shells; stipple brush*

Tip Lightly spritz alcohol inks with alcohol to re-wet ink and achieve a mottled effect.

1 Layer torn vellum pieces over map mounted on cardstock with gloss medium. Stamp bottle on shrink plastic. Stain stamped bottle and vellum background with alcohol inks; move wet inks around with paintbrush using a light pouncing motion; spritz with alcohol to blend and lighten colors. Silhouette cut stamped bottle.

2 Mix ivory acrylic paint with molding paste; add tiny glass marbles for texture. Apply texture around edges of layered vellum with a palette knife; apply heavier in the lower right corner for bottle to rest in.

VARIATION

A cheerful dimensional sunflower (Paper House Productions) sits on top of a combination of unlikely materials: copper screen, molding paste, gingham ribbon and patterned paper (Rusty Pickle).

3 Hold the stamped bottle parallel to the layered design; gently secure in wet sand. Push some of the sand from the lower right corner over the bottom of the bottle; place a few shells under bottle for support until the molding paste dries. Apply quick-drying liquid adhesive along edges of bottle as shown. Carefully bend top edge of bottle back toward vellum layers until the two meet; hold in place until adhesive dries.

4 Press shells into wet molding paste; set aside to dry. Add color to sand texture by stippling with acrylic paints. Place a few more shells and rolled paper behind bottle with tweezers.

Colorant

Here is a simple stamp and paint technique that is sure to be added to your "favorites" list. The fact that this technique is super easy is nothing compared to the spectacular effects you'll create.

Texture

The clean, fresh look of a white-on-white textured collage makes a subtle and elegant statement. If you are new to this type of collage, get ready to push aside a few barriers and gain a new sense of creative freedom.

Image

You don't have to spend hours learning an image-editing program to get the look of hand-painted photos. Instead, infuse your photographs with a variety of colored effects using ink pads and re-inkers.

Collage

This is one design tool I don't think I'll ever abandon. In fact, whenever I find I'm facing the blank page and struggling to start a layout, I always turn to "designing on the grid." Without a doubt, this tool is the little black dress of the graphic design world.

Layout supplies not listed with a technique can be found on page 123.

Essential Elements Diagram

Colorant

Stamped Paint
Imprints

Texture

Molding Paste
Textures

Image

Inked Photo
Effects

Collage

Designing on
the Grid (background)

Colorant

Stamped Paint Imprints

I really like techniques that take away some of the creative pressure we put on ourselves because they don't have to be done perfectly to look great. This acrylic paint technique is one of those techniques, and it produces a beautiful damask-like effect when used with pearlescent paint and a foam stamp. I also like the "re-do-ability" aspect of this technique; if you're not happy with an imprint, brush over the area with more paint and try again!

Foam stamps with deeply carved lines are best for this technique. Work in small areas on a 12 x 12" background; paint and stamp only half of the cardstock at a time because acrylic paint dries quickly.

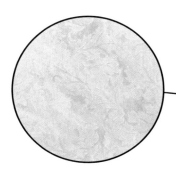

Supplies: *Acrylic paint (Golden); foam stamp; paintbrush*

Tip Work in small areas so that the paint doesn't dry before you make the imprints!

1 Generously apply light blue and pearl acrylic paints on cardstock as shown. Blend colors where they meet, but do not mix colors together. Do not worry about perfect application; just make sure that the paint is thick enough for a clean foam stamp imprint.

2 Let paint set for about 20 to 30 seconds but do not let it dry; press a dry, chunky foam stamp into the wet paint and lift off. Wipe paint off stamp with a paper towel after each imprint for a clean impression. Continue stamping in wet paint; don't be afraid to overlap design.

3 The end result is a beautiful, faux damask look. Set aside to dry.

VARIATIONS

Pink and purple pearlescent colors really bring out the dimensional elements of this technique.

Add a bit of drama! Red and gold glossy paints (Golden) really add the "wow" factor, especially after the addition of a swipe of Rub 'n Buff gold wax (AMACO) and ColorBox black ink (Clearsnap) over the raised areas.

Texture

Molding Paste Textures

If you are new to traditional collage, not quite comfortable with it, or think that "mine will never look like this," then this is the technique that will help you push those thought barriers aside. A white-on-white textured collage is less daunting to create than a collage that includes a variety of color because you don't have to focus on combining elements and colors.

I've simplified the collage process with visuals and provided questions for you to ask yourself when it comes to wondering, "When is it done?"

Before you begin, gather a variety of light-colored images, textured papers and elements (see supplies list for what I've included in this collage). Then take a deep breath and have some fun!

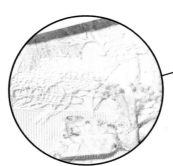

Supplies: *Molding paste, acrylic paint, acrylic matte medium (Golden); dried botanicals (Nature's Pressed, Pressed Petals); foam brush; palette knife; baby wipes; miscellaneous textured and found elements: cheesecloth, glass beads, postage stamps, textured wallpaper, cotton fabric, organza, pearl buttons, ephemera, magazine clippings, orange foil paper, fibers, raffia*

1 Apply three decorative papers and/or images. Think in threes: arrange three papers/images at the points of an imaginary triangle (or draw one like I have!). Brush matte medium on back of paper/images; mount on cardstock. Smooth over paper/images, torn edges and air bubbles with fingertips.

2 Spread molding paste with a palette knife over items mounted in Step 1, as if you were spreading cream cheese on a bagel; smear it on and then scrape some off as shown above. Note: Images above are cropped to show detail.

Tip Turn the collage 90 degrees every once in awhile while adding elements; the new perspective will keep you from thinking too much!

3 Build the collage around the first three mounted items; add one or two textured elements next to items. Apply molding paste over and around each textured element as shown in Step 2. Repeat Steps 1 and 2, alternating the placement of decorative papers, images and textured elements. After four rounds, stop and look at how your collage is progressing; read *How Is It Going?* sidebar. When finished, set aside to dry.

4 Brush white paint over the collage with a foam brush one area at a time; remove excess paint with a baby wipe while paint is still wet. Repeat until entire collage has been painted.

? How Is It Going?

Does any one area look very dark or very light? If YES, add or delete elements to balance those areas. If NO, keep going...

Are there any large empty areas or areas that look too crowded? If YES, add or delete elements, making sure to keep light/dark balance in mind (see question above!). If NO, keep going.

How do I know when it is done? Ah, the question of the hour! This is the toughest question to answer because there is no absolute answer. It is the question only you can answer. So I say, go by your gut feeling.

Still not sure? Here's what I ask myself whenever I'm not sure if a collage is "done:"

Do I like this collage? There is usually something I really like about the collage, and something I don't like. Whatever I don't like, I simply remove! This may be a single element, it may be too much molding paste, or it may be that I don't like how two items look next to each other. The answer to this question is inside of you...it's all about what you like and what you don't like.

Is this collage "missing" something? Usually, there's at least one thing missing; I know this even if I'm not quite sure what that "missing" thing is. For me, the "missing" thing is usually an element that brings order to the chaos. To remedy this, I repeat one element a few times on the collage. In this collage, I chose to mount a vertical line of shell buttons.

Once again, I'll ask myself, Is this collage "missing" something? When the answer is "no," I'm done and I set it aside to dry.

Image
Inked Photo Effects

technique

I love adding unique effects to photographs, especially when I can do it quickly by hand. This technique focuses on how to apply color to inkjet and traditionally processed photos using ink pads and re-inkers.

The soft look of a hand-painted photo can be achieved without taking a lot of time. I like working with Colorbox Cat Eye Chalk ink pads because they are easy to hold and apply directly to paper.

For best results, select black-and-white, sepia or light-colored photos.

Supplies: Gloss fixative spray (Prismacolor); ColorBox chalk ink pads (Clearsnap); cotton swabs; baby wipes

VARIATIONS

Take a look at these variations; you'll be surprised at the cool effects you can achieve with ink pads and re-inkers! Drip re-inkers onto wax paper and then apply with a cosmetic sponge or cotton swab.

Tip Fixative spray is absolutely necessary on ink-jet photos so the photo inks will not smear.

❶ Apply fixative spray if you are working with an inkjet photo. Press ink pad directly onto photo area to be colored; work only one area at a time.

❷ Using a cotton swab, spread ink over desired area. Work from the inside of the photo out toward the edges (I colored my daughter's body first and then the background). Wipe ink from unwanted areas or touch up small areas with a cotton swab. If ink has dried and doesn't remove easily, lightly rub a baby wipe over the area. Spray with fixative when finished and set aside to dry!

Apply one ink at a time, direct to paper. Blot and rub off with tissue while damp in areas to achieve grungy effects. The halftone effect (small dots) is achieved after spraying with fixative spray.

Apply magenta ink over entire photo, spray with fixative and let dry. Get the mottled effect by rubbing some areas with a pre-moistened towelette to remove ink. Start rubbing with light pressure; apply more pressure until desired effect is achieved. Rub copper and black inks around edges.

Apply orange ink to hair with thin paintbrush. Apply blue ink to background; rub with paper towel before ink dries completely. Use same technique with red ink on clothes. Frame image with black ink using the same method.

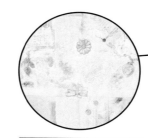

Collage
Designing on the Grid

What do you do when you find yourself facing the blank page, struggling to start a layout? I recommend turning to a tried and true design tool called "designing on the grid." Without a doubt, this tool is like the little black dress of the graphic design world.

The grid is a basic organization tool, providing a sense of order for the elements in your layout. Think of the grid as graph paper; it is a structure for dividing a page into equally sized units. A grid can have nine, 12 or 24 units (or more!); the choice is yours. I suggest starting with a simple 12-unit grid because more grid units mean a more complex design. The elements in your layout—a title, photos or journaling blocks—will take up the units on the grid; they can span two, three or even four units of a grid, depending upon the layout. The grid can not only save you time, it will give your pages a clean, graphic style.

Supplies: Acrylic matte medium (Golden) or PVA; acrylic paint (Golden); foam brush; baby wipes

As you gather the elements for your layout, include a few that will be repeated on the grid. Repetitive elements provide a sense of cohesion to any design. The repetitive elements I selected for this collage are: The Stamped Paint Imprint (page 84), Molding Paste Texture (page 85) and a few pieces of textured wallpaper.

Tips

	stamped imprint	textured collage	textured collage
1	2	3	4
textured collage	stamped imprint	textured wallpaper	
5	6	7	8
stamped imprint	textured wallpaper		
9	10	11	12

① Sketch and plan grid. This grid has four columns and three rows; each unit measures approximately 3½ x 4". Some elements will span two grid units; be sure to measure accordingly.

② Mount repeated elements for units 2, 3, 4, 5, 6, 7, 9, 10 (see Tips). Tear these elements (or papers of choice) into determined unit sizes; mount on cardstock background with matte medium or PVA. Do not worry if the edges go over the lines you've drawn—it makes for a more interesting grid!

VARIATION

Same photos, new look! Colorful, graphic patterned and text papers (American Crafts) are stylishly arranged on a 1" grid. Experiment with shaped elements to fill grid sections; 1" punched circles (Creative Memories) are a fun replacement for squares.

③ Now you can fill the empty sections with whatever you'd like. I've stitched buttons onto fabric and assembled minicollages for units 1, 8, 11 and 12. Add whatever you'd like to these areas; embellish with small decorative elements such as charms, ribbons or beads. Finish with a single horizontal or vertical element, like the grosgrain ribbon, to unify the layout.

④ The last step is to add a single color of paint over the entire collage, giving a sense of cohesion to different elements on the page. Paint over the entire collage with a mix of white and beige. Work in small sections; paint with a foam brush and quickly wipe off with a baby wipe, leaving a washed effect.

Idea Notebook

Textile Textures

Look to fabulous fabrics and notions for unique ways to add texture to your pages.

Copy a favorite patterned paper (American Crafts) onto silk or cotton fabric sheets (Jacquard Prints) made for inkjet printers (below). Form bias tape into a decorative design; adhere to fabric or cardstock with liquid adhesive before stitching (right).

Look for quick and easy options when assembling or securing fabric embellishments; I used staples instead of stitches on the slide mount and pocket (below left). Feed satin ribbon through a needlepoint needle, making stringing buttons, beads and fabric flowers a breeze (right).

Raised Textures

Unique textural effects can be created by building up a surface with materials and mediums or by creating valleys of design by impressing objects into wet mediums.

Gesso & clear silicone caulk

Run decorative comb through wet textures; allow layers to dry in between applications.

Waxed paper

Emboss crumpled wax paper; rub permanent ink pad across cooled surface to accentuate texture.

Molding paste & colored beeswax

Experiment with different types of brushes; stiff brushes create great textured surfaces. Apply texture mediums over images or stenciled designs for interesting effects.

a Do you love to shop? Create your own Fashionista (pattern on page 121) and add your own embellishments!

b A girl can never have too much charm! Create fabulous custom charms with acrylic circles and squares (Heidi Grace Designs) Directions are on page 122.

c Look to the eclectic mix of Bohemian elegance for interesting combinations of brocades and textured materials.

d Infuse black and white with a shock of color for a contemporary twist on a classic look.

e Embellish yourself and your pages with silk and satin ribbons strung with pearls, crystal beads and sequins.

f Add a little ethnic flair to your layouts. Jewelry designs with unique color combinations and patterns can be re-created into distinctive embellishments or page accents.

g Handcrafted details are embellishing everything from jeans to jackets. Create your own embroidered or appliquéd designs with scrapbook and craft supplies.

h Have you noticed how everything shines a little brighter these days? Whether you like a little bit of shine or a lot or sparkle, illuminate your layout with pre-made trims or a scattering of loose sequins.

i Do you go wild for animal prints? Pair animal print paper, ribbon or trim with metallic hardware for an elegant accent. I used a broken hoop earring as my hardware; iron-on gold studs (Cousin Corp.) finish off the look.

j Re-create the look of antique chic with lace seam bindings found in the notions department of fabric stores. Pair with whimsical or floral patterned papers to keep lace looking fresh and contemporary.

k Put a new twist on preppy: Embellish argyle prints with sequins, beads and fibers. Push the look a little more by punching diamond shapes from your favorite patterned papers.

l True blue makes a comeback, which means new color combinations; pair peacock blue with pink or add a little pizazz to navy blue with acid green—whatever the hue, just do the blue!

m Get inspired from today's artistic handbags; take note of your favorite shapes, colors, styles and embellishments and bring those elements into your layouts.

n Allow your inner fashion designer to create an exclusive line of handbags from scraps of patterned papers, ribbon remnants and other fabulous findings.

Tag stickers (EK Success); letter stickers (Creative Imaginations)

a wa... the wild side

PLAY
ball

GAME ★ FACE

4

Image is Everything

Have you ever noticed that scrapbooking begins and ends with an image? A layout begins with a photograph or memory which is transformed with paper and embellishments into a new image—the completed scrapbook page!

Images are visual definitions of something we've seen or experienced. Whether these images are captured on film, or simply mulling around in our brains, they are an essential part of who we are, which is an integral part of our artwork. When it comes to scrapbooking, both the printed image and the memory image become part of our artisitic canvases.

What do you see when you look at an image? Do you see a photo as a finished product, or can you imagine it as art waiting to happen?

Colorant

There is something about the translucent shine of an acrylic glaze that enriches the simplest of surfaces. Glazes can be applied alone or with acrylic paint to achieve brilliant effects while allowing the surface or layer underneath to remain visible.

Texture

How resourceful are you? It's amazing what we can come up with when we don't have something we need to finish a layout. In a pinch, I found that large mailing labels proved to be a worthy surface for assembling a sparkling embellishment.

Image

Imagine if you could create your own rub-on transfers for text, images or designs using your inkjet printer and a piece of transparency. Sound too good to be true? It isn't. It's fabulous!

Collage

There's a cool and innovative style of layered photo art that is emerging from current graphic design trends. This fun technique will push your layouts into the forefront of creative scrapbook trends.

Layout supplies not listed with a technique can be found on page 123.

Colorant
Transparent
Glazes (background)

Texture
Sparkling
Surfaces

Image
Rub-On
Transfers

Collage
Photo
Illustration

Colorant

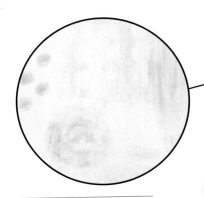

Transparent Glazes

Acrylic glazes enhance painted surfaces the same way that lip gloss enhances a lipstick: with just a hint of color and lots of translucent shine!

Glazes produce brilliant effects while allowing the surface or layer underneath to remain visible, making them perfect for a number of faux paint effects like colorwashing, rag rolling, stippling and sponging.

This quick and carefree technique is created by applying thin layers of colored glazes with a cosmetic sponge. They can be applied alone or with acrylic paints.

Supplies: *Lumiere paints (Jacquard Products); acrylic glazing liquid (Golden); cosmetic sponges; baby wipes*

Tips

- When working with glazes, let each glazed layer dry completely before adding the next.
- Acrylic glazes dry quickly; mix colors with glaze just before applying.

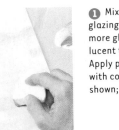

❶ Mix paints with acrylic glazing liquid (1:4 ratio). The more glaze, the more translucent the paint color will be. Apply pink glaze to cardstock with cosmetic sponge as shown; let dry.

❷ Apply yellow glaze over pink glaze with sponge; let dry. Notice how the colors are similar to the look of vellum; they lay over another and create a new shade. Apply turquoise and green glazes in same fashion.

❸ Soften bright colors with white glaze; apply with cosmetic sponge and wipe over background with baby wipes to remove excess paint.

VARIATIONS

Green and blue glazed papers are crafted into a whimsical tag and envelope set. Line envelope with patterned paper (Basic Grey) and punch circles (Creative Memories) before folding into envelope shape.

Paint a quick and easy striped background with metallic glazes and a cosmetic sponge. Patterned paper (SEI)

Texture
Sparkling Surfaces

Time for a little sparkle and shine! If you're looking to add a fabulous texture to your layout, this quick and easy technique is perfect for your favorite sparkly elements—sequins, glitter, tiny glass marbles and seed beads—whatever you choose, just "bling it on!"

The first time I tried this technique, I ran out of double-sided tape. Desperate, I went into resource mode and pulled out a box of Avery mailing labels. Amazingly, the mailing labels worked really well as an adhesive surface and they are much more cost-effective than wide double-stick tape. Secure it to your work surface with re-positionable adhesive; you will need to keep both hands free to hold the embossing gun and add more elements at the same time!

Supplies: *Sequins (Gutermann); fusible fibers (Stampendous!); rainbow sparkle embossing powder (Ranger); pearl UTEE (Suze Weinberg); mailing labels or self-stick sheets; clear tiny glass marbles; embossing gun*

Embellish a cool Artist Trading Card! Layer images or ephemera before surrounding with embellishments. Sequins; beads; ribbon (SEI); decorative metal corner (Nunn Design); buttons (found); glitter glue (Ranger); flower beads (Beadery); colored crystal lacquer; vintage playing card

1 Secure the mailing label sticky side up on a nonstick heat sheet or on a sheet of cardstock with re-positionable adhesive. Sprinkle sequins and clear tiny glass marbles; make sure to leave room for the next item. Shake off excess before adding the next elements.

2 Press fusible fibers onto label. Sprinkle entire surface with sparkle embossing powder; shake off excess and heat with embossing gun.

3 While surface is hot, add another light coating of sparkle embossing powder as well as a sprinkle of pearl UTEE, but don't shake off excess. Heat label from underneath to set powders and then finish by heating on top.

VARIATIONS

Make a sparkling flower in minutes. Sprinkle glitter over a flower stencil before adding tiny glass marbles and embossing powders. (This is a label too!)

Image
Rub-On Transfers

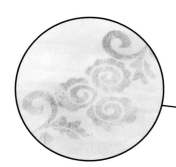

Rub-on transfers are one of the hottest products to hit the scrapbook market in the past year. Imagine creating your own rub-on transfers for text, images and designs with your inkjet printer and a piece of transparency…it's true, and it's so easy to do!

Inkjet transparencies have two sides: a textured surface that holds the ink and prevents smearing as well as a smooth surface that is formally known as the "wrong" side. Printing on the wrong side of an inkjet transparency allows wet ink to sit on the surface, allowing it to be transferred to another surface.

All of the graphic images in this layout have been transferred onto tissue paper using this technique. Tissue paper is the best surface to transfer on because the ink seeps into it and it becomes transparent when it is mounted with acrylic gloss medium. Imagine the possibilities. Your own custom-made rub-ons whenever you want them!

Supplies: *All images/designs on this layout are from Mac type fonts I downloaded free from the Internet. Fonts (Butterflies, Designer Stuff, Ornamental Corners, Ornamental Decorations II all from dafont.com); acrylic gloss medium (Golden); fixative spray (Prismacolor); white tissue paper; foam brush; spoon or palette knife*

Tips

• While creating your own rub-ons, position fingers close to image while rubbing to prevent the transfer from moving.

• Spritz transparency with alcohol and wipe off after a transfer; now you're ready for another one!

1 Print type or design onto smooth or "wrong" side of transparency, printing type, photo or design in reverse.

2 Quickly place transparency onto tissue paper ink side down. Hold transparency firmly on the tissue paper with one hand and press over design/image with fingertips so ink will seep into tissue. Burnish over entire design with a palette knife or back of a spoon. Lift transparency to see your transfer!

3 Spray tissue paper with fixative before mounting so inks don't run; let dry. Tear excess tissue paper from around design/image. Apply a thin coat of acrylic gloss medium to cardstock with foam brush; place transferred image on wet gloss medium. Apply more gloss medium on top of tissue paper; smooth out any bubbles or creases with fingers or foam brush.

Transfer an image onto a thin coat of regular gel medium applied on cardstock instead of tissue paper for more vibrant colors and clarity.

VARIATIONS

Image printed on tissue paper and mounted on cardstock.

Collage

Photo Illustration

technique

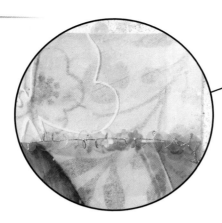

Graphic design trends influence everything that has a visual presence in society, including advertising, fashion, electronics…even scrapbooking! The bounty of geometric prints and vibrant colors on paper and embellishment products are great examples of today's popular graphic trend.

One trend that has really caught my eye is called photo illustration. This cool blend of image and illustration translates into some fabulously creative ideas for photo art. Simple line drawings and silhouette figures indicative of this style don't require you to be an illustrator. If you can trace around or over an image, you can create this cool!

Supplies: Transparency; fine-point white paint pen (Sharpie)

VARIATIONS

❶ Print or copy designs 30 percent smaller and 30 percent larger than sizes mounted on painted background (see opposite page). Trace outline of design onto transparency sheet with white paint pen.

Create a stylish portrait fit for a queen! Trace silhouette of enlarged copy onto colored vellum; mount over text or related ephemera. Patterned paper (Provo Craft); letter stickers (K & Company); miscellaneous ephemera.

❷ Layer transparency over background and mount.

Nervous about drawing on your photo? Trace lines and details onto a piece of transparency layered over photo. Black pen lines and colored crystal lacquer are easy ways to incorporate photo illustration elements.

Colorant

Today's metallic mix of colors is adding an illuminating effect to all kinds of accents and embellishments. Infuse your photographs with a hint of metallic shimmer with alluring yet effortless techniques.

Texture

Gel medium textures have a way of inviting the touch and intriguing the eye. Their ability to hold shape encourages your imagination to draw, comb, shape, stamp or imprint a unique textured surface.

Image

Here's a chance to add to your library of image-transfer techniques. With three techniques to choose from, you can create cool and interesting effects no matter your artistic level.

Collage

You don't have to know how to use image-editing software to create a transparent photo montage. Look to your photos for design opportunities that can be created with a color copier.

Layout supplies not listed with a technique can be found on page 123.

Essential Elements Diagram

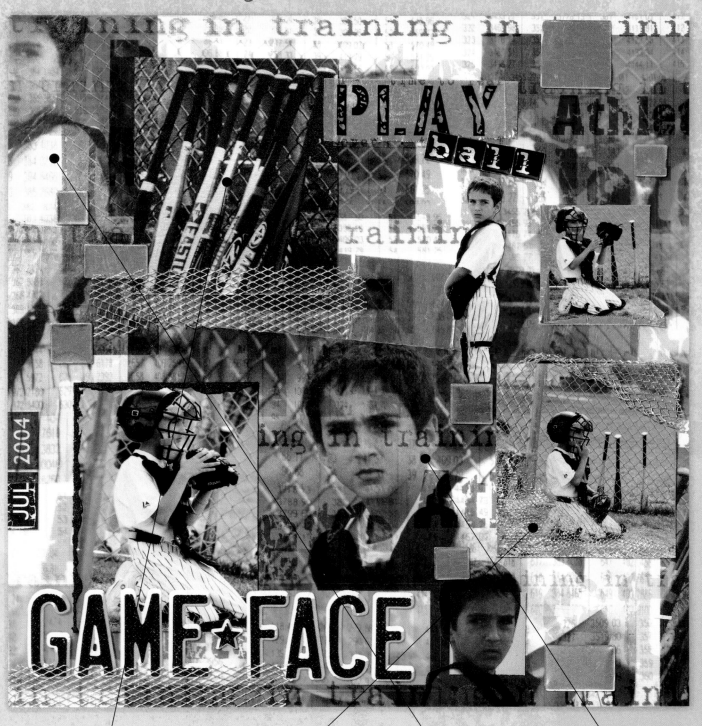

Colorant	Texture	Image	Collage
Metallic Photo Effects	Gel Medium Imprints	Photo Transfers	Transparency Montage (background)

Colorant

Metallic Photo Effects

A metallic rainbow has cast its multihued spectrum upon all things decorative in surface design. So why not add an understated glow to your photos? Choose from four quick and easy techniques; each results in a different effect but they all add a little luster to your photos. Take your pick, and bring out the glowing qualities in your images.

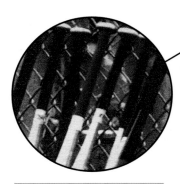

Supplies: *Metallic paint pen (Krylon); wax crayons (Inoxcrom); transparency; metallic cardstock; acrylic paint; metallic rub-ons; fixative spray*

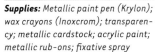

Transparency Overlay
Mount photo transparency onto metallic cardstock with spray adhesive.

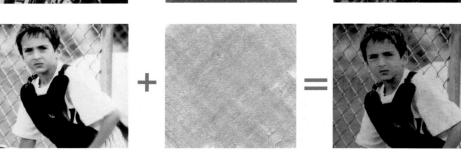

Painted Transparency
Color with metallic paint pen (Krylon) or paint two coats of acrylic paint on **back of** transparency.

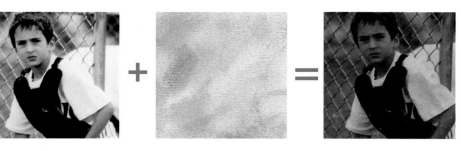

Metallic Rub-Ons
Rub metallic color directly onto photo; lightly blend and buff with tissue. Create a warm glow by using gold for skin tones. Finish with fixative spray.

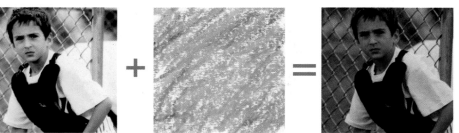

Wax Crayons
Scribble wax crayon on processed photo; give a quick shot of heat with embossing gun (no more than seven to eight seconds!). Lightly blot with tissue to blend colors. Color around edges with crayon; heat five seconds with embossing gun (do not blend!). Finish with fixative spray.

Texture
Gel-Medium Imprints

How about making a good impression? Imprint your style and make a textured statement with decorative stamps or unique dimensional elements pressed into acrylic gel medium. Gel-medium textures have a way of inviting a touch and intriguing the eye, and their ability to hold shape invites your imagination to play.

I made my impression on a photograph using metal mesh and metallic rub-ons. Whether you spell out a subtle message with foam stamps or decide to imprint a design, gel medium textures will have you making a great impression.

Supplies: Regular acrylic gel medium (Golden); metal mesh (AMACO); metallic rub-ons (Robin); palette knife

It's good to be the queen! Press rubber stamp (Inkadinkado) into wet gel medium; let sit for one minute and remove. Add glowing effects with metallic rub-ons when dry.

VARIATIONS

① Apply gel medium with a palette knife along the side and bottom of photo.

② Press the mesh into gel medium. Apply more gel medium over mesh as shown. Let sit for eight to 10 minutes, but make sure to remove mesh before the gel medium dries!

③ Apply silver wax rub-ons with fingertips over gel texture to enhance imprint.

Reinforce the excitement of an action photo by drawing wavy lines with a decorative comb (Delta) above and below the focal point. Sprinkle glitter onto wet gel medium.

Impressed by the city...letter stamps, permanent pen ink (Sharpie) and paint pens (Krylon) express a colorful city life.

Image
Photo/Image Transfers

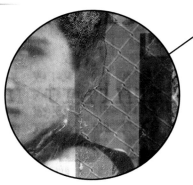

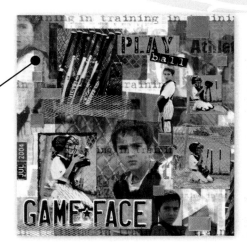

I think photo transfers are extremely addicting. The three techniques featured here provide something for everyone, no matter your artistic level. Each technique produces a different result and uses different materials and methods of transfer.

Create a translucent strip of photos on tape, work a little magic with a heated iron or make a clear, dimensional photo "skin." Whatever method you choose, one of them is sure to be a permanent addition to your library of photo-transfer techniques. Plan for unexpected results when working with image transfers; they are a serendipitous technique that isn't about perfection!

Supplies: *Clear packing tape (Quickstick); water in spritzer bottle*

2 Iron-On Transfer

Make a montaged image with purchased transfer paper and a heat tool or iron. Print image on transfer paper. Place transfer paper facedown over image printed on cardstock. Slowly rub heat tool or iron over back of transfer; press firmly as you move heat tool over back of image. Let cool for approximately 30 seconds; lift transfer paper off to reveal image.

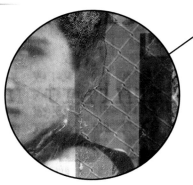

1 Packing-Tape Transfer

Lift off a vertical image or succession of horizontal images with clear packing tape.

1 Adhere the packing tape over freshly printed inkjet or color copy image. (This works great with magazine images, too!) Turn over and firmly burnish back of image with fingertips or other smooth object; set aside for about 10 minutes.

2 Turn image back over, paper side up. Spritz with water and begin rubbing over paper with fingertips to remove paper.

3 Continue spritzing with water and rubbing over paper with fingers, removing paper from back of image until clean. Allow taped image to dry before mounting.

3 Gel-Skin Tranfer

Show off a star athlete! Place color-copied image on wax paper, image side up. Spread a coat of gel medium (approximately $1/8$" thick) over image as shown. Set aside to dry; move on to next step when gel medium is completely clear. Remove paper from back of image as described in Packing-Tape Transfer. When clean, adhere over newspaper (or other surface) as shown with gloss or matte medium.

Collage

Transparency Montage

We all love having options, whether we're talking about colorant techniques, image transfers or flavors of ice cream. When it comes to techniques, options and variations give you a choice of looks, materials used and the amount of time you spend creating them.

Keeping with that thought, this montaged background has been created from a few photos that have provided a number of image options. With the help of a color copier (or printer), these photos have been cropped, enlarged, copied, toned or reversed to produce a variety of different images. Take a look at two of the photos and their variations used in this montage and translate the copying techniques to your own photos.

Supplies: *Text transparency (Creative Imaginations)*

Here are a few key words to look for on a color copier to re-create a variety of looks:

- Vary color: Find "single color" and select green.
- Flip image: Find "invert" or "mirror image."
- Change size: "Reduce" or "enlarge."
- Lighten or darken: Find "variable color balance" (to change density of color); select lighter or darker depending upon preference.

This photo provided two images: an enlarged player for the packing-tape transfer (left) and an enlarged and reversed player for a water-decal transfer (above).

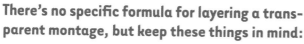

There's no specific formula for layering a transparent montage, but keep these things in mind:

- Scale: Think small, medium and large (from page 21).
- Color value: Light and dark images (from page 51).
- Remember to vary the light and dark images as well as large and small images when layering a transparent montage.

Look to your photos for elements that can be enlarged and integrated into your layout. This photo provided three images: an enlarged fence, an enlarged catcher and an enlarged color-toned print of the baseball bats.

Colorant

This unique colorant technique will have you blending patterned papers into designs which resemble the smooth look of digital collages. Gather together a fabulous collection of patterned papers and your sense of adventure before trying this technique!

Texture

Creating a dimensional textured effect on the architectural photos in this layout seemed like the best way to pay homage to the grand artistry of Chicago's treasured skyline.

Image

The art of altering photos has reached new heights with a cool photo-bleaching technique. Whether soaked, stamped or scrubbed, bleached photo effects are truly a unique way to artistically alter your photos.

Collage

The power of the written word has become a prominent element of page design. While there are no hard and fast rules, there are a few things to keep in mind when collaging words so that your text won't look like a serving of alphabet soup!

Layout supplies not listed with a technique can be found on page 123.

Colorant
Patterned Paper Transfer

Texture
Architextural Images

Image
Photo Bleaching

Collage
Letter and Word Collage

Colorant

Patterned Paper Transfer

Throughout this book you've seen many ways to apply, layer and integrate color onto paper. This last colorant technique is a step beyond the others: transferring patterned paper onto another surface.

After working with photo and image transfers, I couldn't help but wonder if patterned paper would transfer onto another surface. The answer is yes! Why would you want to transfer patterned paper onto another surface? A patterned paper transfer results in a blended design that looks as if it has melted into the surface it is transferred on. This is different from simply layering torn papers because the transfer becomes one with the background. I think it closely resembles the cool look of blended digital collages.

And here's a bonus! This is the same technique used for transferring images onto solid or patterned papers!

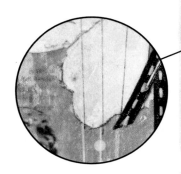

Supplies: *Patterned paper (American Crafts); soft gel medium (Golden); cardstock*

Tips

Practice makes perfect! When creating patterned paper transfers, too much water and too much pressure rubbing can result in the transfer rubbing off. Adjust fingertip pressure according to type of paper transfer is printed on; thin copy paper requires a much lighter touch than a thick photo paper.

VARIATIONS

Patterned papers (Basic Grey) blend seamlessly over an image transfer.

1 Trim patterned paper about 1½" larger than desired size. Apply a generous layer of gel medium on patterned paper; turn over and place facedown onto surface that is receiving the transfer. Gently press and smooth out air bubbles with fingers, but do not press so hard that gel oozes out from between the layers. Let sit for approximately 10 to 15 minutes.

2 Lift corner of image to see if image has transferred. If so, slowly pull up corner of patterned paper. (If not, leave alone and try again in five more minutes.) Only some of the paper will peel off easily at this time, so don't worry if it doesn't all come off!

3 When gel medium is dry, remove the balance of paper by lightly spritzing with water and gently rubbing paper with fingertips in a circular motion. As paper curls and comes off under your fingertips, image will begin to appear; repeat until image is clean. Have patience with this part of the technique; it can be a little messy but is worth the effort and cleanup! Seal image with a thin coat of gel medium.

A photo transfer stands tall amongst patterned paper designs.

Texture
Architextural Images

I am always looking for ways that I can get a "look" without having to spend a whole lot of time learning a new technique. When I came across a multileveled and layered sculptural piece, my mind instantly thought how cool it would be to bring a dimensional image to a scrapbook layout. After experimenting with tissue paper, foam core, light-weight plaster and molding paste, I realized that creating an "architextural" image can be simple or complex depending upon the materials used.

We're going for simple here, so before you say "I can't draw like that," please know that I can't either; I am not an illustrator! I am a really good tracer, though, and I bet you are too. Adding layers of tissue paper over a photo builds texture and dimension while maintaining a transparent image that is perfect for tracing over! In fact, this technique is not much more than a step beyond the photo illustration technique on page 99.

Supplies: *Acrylic gloss medium (Golden); fine-point pen (Sharpie); pink tissue paper*

VARIATIONS

Bring an adventure photo to life with molding paste texture and a tissue paper transfer. Apply molding paste over foreground rocks; let dry. Mount tissue paper transfer over dried molding paste with matte medium.

❶ Apply thin layer of acrylic gloss medium over photo. Layer pink tissue paper on wet gloss medium. Apply a second coat of gloss medium. Repeat with five to six layers of tissue paper in shades of pink. Add as many layers of tissue paper as long as you can still see the underlying image. Set aside to dry.

❷ Outline image with a fine-point pen. Draw as much detail as you want or simply outline the image. Light, loose pen strokes will create the look of a professional illustration!

Add dimension to a stamped faux fresco design with torn layers built up with molding paste.

Image

Photo Bleaching

While the idea of bleaching your photos may seem crazy, keep in mind that photographers use a number of chemicals to develop and create unique photographic effects—chemicals with huge warning labels on them!

The outer layers of a photo (the emulsion) serves as the photo's protective coat. The emulsion can be manipulated and chemically treated to produce a variety of exciting and unique results. Bleaching is a great primer for enhancing photos with colorants such as stains, dyes, and oil or acrylic paints.

This technique works with either black-and-white or color photos, and regularly processed or inkjet photos. However, you will get different results with each type of photo (see below).

Please use this technique for a fun effect on a copy of a photo. I am not a professional photographer and do not know about the archival quality of a bleached photo.

Supplies: *Two glass bowls; water; household bleach; plastic or plastic-coated tongs (not metal); timer; clothespin or other type of clip*

Tips

• Immerse a test photo for 12 to 15 seconds and then adjust the time up or down depending upon the effect you want.

• Be prepared for a different result every time you bleach a photo; one second more or one second less in bleach will change the look of a photo.

1 Set out two bowls (larger than photo); one for bleach + water mix and one for water (called a "bath"). Place paper towels under the bath bowl. Fill the first bowl with a ratio of 1:7 bleach or 1 ounce of bleach to 7 ounces of water. Fill the bath bowl half full with water.

2 Set timer for 12 to 15 seconds for processed photos. For inkjet photos, set timer for 10 to 12 seconds. Using tongs, place photo in bleach + water mix; turn on timer. Gently shake or agitate the bowl and watch the photo's color begin to float away from the edges of the photo. When the timer goes off...

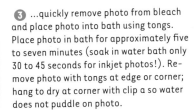

3 ...quickly remove photo from bleach and place photo into bath using tongs. Place photo in bath for approximately five to seven minutes (soak in water bath only 30 to 45 seconds for inkjet photos!). Remove photo with tongs at edge or corner; hang to dry at corner with clip a so water does not puddle on photo.

VARIATIONS

I love the hazy, vintage effect that resulted from bleaching this black-and-white photo of a tractor that was printed on my inkjet printer; this is perfect for enhancing with inks!

Notice the soft edges around this processed black-and-white photo? Bleaching it resulted in a faded, purplish tone.

Collage

Letter/Word Collage

The art of the written word has a bold presence on today's scrapbook pages due to the vast number of letter stamps and stickers, printed text designs, rub-ons and type fonts available. For this technique however, I'm going to focus on the way to layer a letter or word collage no matter the medium used.

The title on this featured layout is a combination of stamped, stenciled and handwritten words layered on top and around another. When it comes to layering letters or words over one another, there are a few things to keep in mind so that your finished product won't look like a serving of alphabet soup!

When layering type, pay attention to the scale (size) and color value (light and dark) of the elements that are being combined. Vary the size and color of the type so that the elements work together instead of fighting one another. Notice how the four-layer title starts with the biggest and lightest font in the background and gets smaller and darker with each layer.

Supplies: *Letter stamps (Li'l Davis Designs, Making Memories); Color-Box white, black and magenta ink pads (Clearsnap); gold leaf paint pen (Krylon); letter stencil, black paint pen (EK Success); letter stamp (Memories in the Making)*

Words bloom into art! Enlarge foam stamp (Duncan) design on a copier. Silhouette cut sections and mount on cardstock; build collage right over silhouette-cut sections from found magazine text.

Variations

Stamp large letters in white ink.

Write script letters with gold paint pen.

Write letters using stencil and black pen.

Stamp small words in black, white and magenta inks.

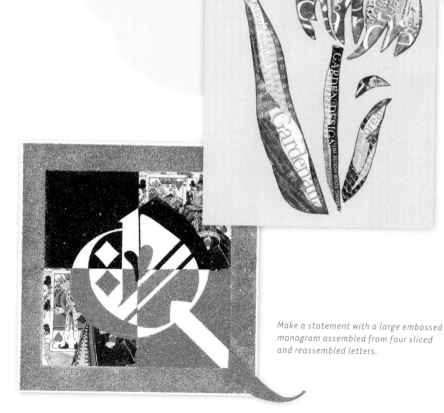

Make a statement with a large embossed monogram assembled from four sliced and reassembled letters.

Embellished Images

Change the look of an image by changing the embellishments.

Modern Bohemian

Create large sheer flowers by copying patterned paper (Frances Meyer) onto plain vellum. Change color of letter stickers (Creative Imaginations) using pens before coating with clear UTEE (crack when cool).

Shabby Chic

Enhance the look by adding chalk and glitter-glue details to flower stickers (K & Company). Apply crackled paint product (Delta) onto photo with acrylic paint for distressed effect.

Deco Design

For deco design, keep facial features together in one grid segment for a pleasing focal point. Layer grid over patterned vellums to soften area between photo segments.

Get the Look

Unique Photo Effects

Vignette

A vignette is a popular photo effect where the photo gradually fades into a dark-colored background. Create this look with ink pads and a stipple brush; lightly stipple white and silver ink around perimeter of photo. Rub along edges with black ink for a dark finish.

Stained Photos

Believe it or not, you can change the color of a regularly processed photo with coffee, tea, red wine or food coloring! Choose a light black-and-white photo. Set up area similar to the bleaching technique on page 110. Replace bleach with 10 to 12 drops of blue food coloring in 20 oz. of water; soak for 15 to 20 minutes and then rinse in water bath.

Faux Fresco

Re-create the look of an aged plastered image with a photo transfer onto a textured paint product called Paper Perfect (Deco Art). See page 108 for image transfer technique.

Lomography

Capture the action as it happens with a unique camera called a Lomo. Originally from Russia, a Lomo camera creates exceptionally vivid, high-contrast photos. My Lomo has four lenses which captures four images with the push of one button...so cool I can't stand it! Check out what Lomo cameras are all about at www.lomography.com.

Faux Polaroid Transfer & Emulsion Lift

Create the look of two alternative photographic processes known as a Polaroid transfer (right photo) and a Polaroid emulsion lift (left photo) using an inkjet printer. Turn to page 123 for directions.

IMAGE IS EVERYTHING

Altered Images

1 *Architecture: Draw up some cool effects with a bleach pen (Clorox).*

2 *Glowing Witch: Give a transparent image sparkle and shine.*

3 *Dreamy Pigeons: Combine gel medium and acrylic paint for a two-toned image transfer.*

4 *Chicago: Create a unique signature with a bleach pen (Clorox).*

5 *Miss Trixie: Use alcohol inks to creat a mottled photo border.*

6 *Winter Wonderland: Enhance a photo with inked and embossed effects.*

7 *Orchids: Create an abstract vignette with metallic inks.*

8 *Country Girl: Add an artistic touch with a grunge brushed border.*
9 *Peacock Feather: Create a cyanotype (with pre-treated paper) in the sun! Letter stickers (Creative Imaginations)*
Refer to page 123 for directions to all photo techniques.

Emerging From the Layers

A Photographic Challenge

Throughout this book you've seen how incredibly rich and dimensional the art of collage can be. The relationship between the layers of elements and the layers of you are evident on the pages of your scrapbooks when the colors, textures and images of our lives blend into artistic layers of meaning. Now that you have reached the end of this book, it is time for you to emerge from the layers and allow someone to document you. Why? Because the layers of your family's life are incomplete if they don't include you!

So here is the challenge: Hand the camera over to a member of your family, a best friend, a loved one or a child...and ask him or her to take pictures of things that remind that person of you (18 to 24 photos). You will see yourself through the eyes of someone who loves you and maybe see yourself in a whole new way! You may want to put together a small album or journal of these photos; not only will you have a wonderful collection of personal photos you'll also have a meaningful collection of images that speaks volumes about the person who took them.

And just in case you're wondering if I took my own challenge...I did. I handed the camera over to my 10-year-old daughter, Rachel. She loved having the opportunity to photograph things that reminded her of me, and she was proud that her point of view was important enough to be documented. I will forever treasure the photographs she took of "me" because I can now appreciate her open heart and how she sees beauty in the ordinary; where I see disorganized piles of magazines, she sees me learning. Where I see a tired mom working on a deadline, she sees me as incredibly happy doing what I love.

How different everything looks when you see yourself through the eyes of another! Enjoy the new perspective...and all the many layers of you!

Patterns

Use these convenient patterns for trying out some of the techniques featured in this book. Simply enlarge the patterns on a photocopier and print onto paper or cardstock.

Realistic Object Collage, page 27

Abstract Photo Collage, page 33

Dimensional Decoupage, page 75

Fashionable Inspirations, page 90

Additional Instructions & Credits

Pages 16-21 Buster Brown
Additional page supplies: Patterned papers (SEI); digital collage of images printed on transparency, polka-dot stamp (Hero Arts); gold brads; letter stickers (Doodlebug Design); white acrylic paint (Golden); brown inkpad (Clearsnap); metal dog tag (Boxer Scrapbook Productions); rub-on letters (Li'l Davis Designs); link chain

Texture technique: Cardstock; white tissue paper; acrylic gloss medium (Golden); brown chalk ink pads (Clearsnap); watermark ink pad; clear embossing powder (Stamp 'n Stuff); clear UTEE (Suze Weinberg); embossing gun; gold embossing foil (Stampendous!)

Variation supplies: Patterned paper (Anna Griffin, Far and Away); printed transparency (Creative Imaginations)

Pages 22-27 Something About Mary
Additional page supplies: Patterned papers (Deluxe Designs, Hot Off The Press, KI Memories, Scrapbook Wizard, SEI); acrylic paint (Golden); masking tape

Image technique: Circle punch (Creative Memories); regular gloss medium (Golden); brown chalk ink pad (Clearsnap)

Collage technique: Sharp scissors

Variation supplies: Patterned papers (Bo-Bunny Press)

Pages 28-33 All American Girl
Additional page supplies: Letter stickers (American Crafts, Making Memories); patterned papers (Bo-Bunny Press, Flair Designs); buttons, nailheads (my own); ribbon (Me & My Big Ideas)

Collage technique: Abstract design pattern on page 120; textured cardstock, double-sided tape, buttons

Pages 34-39 Riding a Wave
Colorant Technique: White cardstock (glossy or coated paper will produce a different effect); dye ink re-inkers (Clearsnap); alcohol in spritzer; brayer; gesso or white acrylic paint; baby wipes; foam brush

Variation supplies: Buttons

Image technique: Double-sided adhesive; craft knife

Pages 42-43 Get the Look: Pop Art
3 Metal circles (Heidi Grace Designs)
5 Patterned papers (Me & My Big Ideas)
6 Apple iPod silhouette image how-to (http://www.macmerc.com/articles/Graphics_Tips/260) 10 Word stickers (Making Memories)

Title supplies: Letter and number stickers (American Crafts, Creative Imaginations, Li'l Davis Designs, SEI, Sticker Studio); stencil letters (C-Thru Ruler)

Pages 52-57 How Many Times
Additional page supplies: Patterned paper (Provo Craft); silver paint pen (Krylon); text stamp (Coronado Island Stamping); acrylic paint, gel medium (Golden); buttons; organza ribbon, velvet ribbon (Offray); decorative scissors; vellum; sequins; tiny glass marbles; straight pin

Variation supplies: Acrylic paints (Golden); glitter paint (Stewart Gill)

Texture technique: Silver paint pen (Krylon)

Image technique: White ink, chalk inks (Clearsnap)

Collage technique: Acrylic paints, matte medium (Golden); quick-dry liquid adhesive (Duncan); copyright-free clip art; sturdy cardstock; craft knife; paintbrush; cardboard; hemp string

Variation supplies: Acrylic paint (Golden); self-adhesive foam shapes (Fibre Crafts)

Pages 58-63 Alex
Additional page supplies: Miscellaneous hardware

Colorant technique: Patterned papers (Flair Designs, Frances Meyer); circle punch (Creative Memories); acrylic glazing liquid (Golden); letter stamps (Making Memories, Rubber Stampede); chalk inkpads (Clearsnap); artist's masking tape; alcohol in spritzer bottle

Pages 66-67 Get the Look
1 Circle punch (Creative Memories); daisy punch (Marvy/Uchida)
3 Stencil Technique: A decorative stencil (Delta) is one of the easiest ways to create the look of a screenprint. Whether the design is filled in with acrylic ink (Speedball) as mine is, or you use the stencil to create just an outline of a shape, take a new look at today's stenciled designs.
4 Sticker Mask Technique: Adhere letter stickers (SEI) onto patterned paper; brayer over with acrylic paint. Cut to size; trim with corner rounder and decorative scissors before mounting on patterned paper (SEI). Adhere butterfly sticker (source unknown) onto patterned paper (SEI); silhouette cut. Remove sticker with un-du adhesive remover; ink edges with black ink pad and mount over letters as shown.
5 Leaves font (http://www.100megsfree.com/lime/dings.htm)
7 Tree branch clip art (http://www.freewebs.com/stencilry/)
8 Trace Magazine Images: Place tracing paper over image; trace outline with pencil. Copy or scan and print onto patterned or colored paper; silhouette cut.

Pages 70-75 The Princess & The Pea
Additional page supplies: Flower button (Junkitz); tulle; fabric; mini brads; miscellaneous buttons

Colorant technique: Patterned paper; gel medium or PVA

Collage technique: Paper yarn (Making Memories)

Page 76-81 Time In A Bottle
Additional page supplies: Printed transparency (Creative Imaginations); satin ribbon (Offray); gold studs (Cousin Corp.)

Texture technique: Non-stick craft sheet

Variation supplies: Molding paste (Golden); twigs (7 Gypsies); eyelets; polka dot ribbon; vellum; can lid

Pages 82-87 Where Did the Time Go?
Additional page supplies: Wood appliqué (Artistic Appliques); glass leaf beads (Cousin Corp.); grosgrain ribbon (SEI); hooks and eyes; glass beads; shell buttons; textured wallpaper; cotton fabric; wire heart charm; metallic thread; dried daisies; gypsum

Colorant technique: Foam stamp (source unknown)

Page 90-91 Get the Look
Lucky Charms: Punch patterned paper, images, text or printed transparency into shapes. Adhere with Diamond Glaze; set aside to dry. Apply two layers of Diamond Glaze; allow each layer to dry before applying the next. Remove excess diamond glaze in hole with manicure stick; attach jump ring. Paint around edges with gold paint pen

Pages 94-99 Sweet Baby J
Additional page supplies: Metal-rimmed tag (Making Memories); sequins; embroidery floss; tulle

Variation #1 (Colorant technique)—supplies: Acrylic paint (Golden)

Variation #2 (Texture technique)—supplies: Glitter (Magic Scraps); embossing powder (Stampendous!); flower stencil (Delta)

Variation supplies (Image technique)—supplies: Regular gel medium (Golden); colored pencils

Variation #1 (Collage technique)—supplies: Colored crystal lacquer

Variation #2 (Collage technique)—supplies: Foil crown; playing card

Pages 100-105 Game Face
Additional page supplies: Printed transparency (Creative Imaginations); metal tiles (Heidi Grace Designs); metal repair tape (3M); acrylic paints, molding paste (Golden); letter stickers (Creative Imaginations, Sticker Studio)

Image technique: Regular gel medium (Golden); iron-on transfer (Hewlett-Packard); waxed paper; water spritzer bottle

Pages 106-111 Chicago
Additional page supplies: Gold paint pen (Krylon); ribbon (Offray); foam letter stamps (Making Memories); ornamental foam stamp (Delta); metallic ink re-inkers (Clearsnap); gold rub-ons (Autumn Leaves); pink tissue paper; stapler; gold ink

Variation supplies: Patterned paper (KI Memories); gold paint pen (Krylon)

Variation #2 supplies: embossing paper; embossing powders (Stampendous!, Stamp 'n Stuff)

Page 114 Faux Polaroid Transfer & Emulsion Lift
Faux Transfer: Print photo on glossy photo paper. Immerse in warm water for 5-10 seconds; lift out and place face down on textured cardstock. Cover with a hand towel and press heated iron over image for about 20-30 seconds. Emulsion Lift: Print image on quick-dry inkjet transparency. Soak in warm water for about 10-15 seconds; gently separate film with image on it from transparency. Place cardstock in water under floating film and lift up out of water. Gently smooth out wet filmy image with fingers; set aside to dry. Add colorant of choice after image dries.

Page 116-117 Get the Look
Altered Photos (directions)
1 Architecture: Scribble over photo with wide tip of bleach pen (Clorox); Draw random design; let sit on (a) inkjet photo for 1-2 minutes or (b) processed photo for 5-7 minutes. Rinse off under running water; gel consistency of product needs force of water from faucet. Hang photo by corner to dry.

2 Glowing Witch: Print photo on transparency; do not trim to size yet. Turn over and coat back of image with acrylic gloss medium (or Modge Podge, crystal lacquer); sprinkle glitter on wet medium. Layer torn pieces of colored tissue paper onto wet medium. Apply second coat of gloss medium and set aside to dry; trim photo to size.

3 Dreamy Pigeons: Apply plain acrylic gel medium and paint mixed with gel medium over copy of photo to transfer. Place image face down on printed transparency (Creative Imaginations). Follow steps 2 and 3 on p. 108 to complete transfer. Adhere gold foil paper behind transparency; scratch with craft knife to remove areas of foil.

4 Chicago: Write with thin tip of bleach pen (Clorox); let sit on (a) inkjet photo for 1-2 minutes or (b) processed photo for 5-7 minutes. Rinse off under running water; gel consistency of product needs force of water from faucet. Hang photo by corner to dry.

5 Miss Trixie: Print photo on shrink plastic but do not shrink! Work in small sections: spritz around edges of photo with alcohol. Add a drop or two of colored alcohol ink; dab ink and move around with paintbrush. Allow photo to dry flat.

6 Winter Wonderland: Turn a drab before photo (small inset) to a beautiful textured image. If using inkjet photo, spray fixative before starting technique. Add inks (ColorBox chalk inks by Clearsnap) to sky of processed photo using technique on page 86. Spray photo with fixative (Prismacolor); set aside to dry. Press Versamark ink pad over photo; sprinkle pearl UTEE over entire photo. Shake off excess and heat making sure to not concentrate heat on photo for more than a few seconds at a time. Press ink pad in certain areas to build up texture: sprinkle UTEE sparkle embossing powder and heat again. A few blisters may develop on photo as shown here but the more coats of UTEE, the less chance of blistering.

7 Orchids: Apply layers of ink (ColorBox Mica Magic Re-inkers – Pearl, Black, Sugar Plum by Clearsnap) one color at

a time with a quick swipe around focal point; apply with a cosmetic sponge. Let dry completely. Remove some of the inked areas by rubbing a baby wipe in a circular motion over photo. When you have achieved desired effects, set aside dry. Finish with pearl ink lightly applied over background and around edges of photo.

8 Country Girl: Refer to page 54 for Grunge Brush Technique. While paint is still wet, Remove paint from focal points; wipe with baby wipe while paint is still damp. Set aside to dry. To remove more paint: dampen photo by wiping with another baby wipe. Apply brush strokes on photo in same fashion using a clean brush. NOTE: Spray inkjet photos with fixative and let dry before doing technique.

9 Peacock Feather: A cyanotype is a blue printed image which is created outside of the darkroom using chemically treated paper (Sunprint Kit, Lawrence Hall of Science). Place flat items like leaves, feathers, keys, etc. on sunprint paper; place clear acrylic sheet over item and place in sun for a few minutes. Rinse paper off in water for about 1 minute and dry flat.

Sources

The following companies manufacture products featured in this book. Please check your local retailers to find these materials, or go to a company's Web site for the latest product. In addition, we have made every attempt to properly credit the items mentioned in this book. We apologize to any company that we have listed incorrectly, and we would appreciate hearing from you.

3M
(800) 364-3577
www.3m.com
7 Gypsies
(800) 588-6707
www.7gypsies.com
American Art Clay Co. (AMACO)
(800) 374-1600
www.amaco.com
American Crafts
(801) 226-0747
www.americancrafts.com
Anna Griffin, Inc.
(888) 817-8170
www.annagriffin.com
Anthropologie- no contact info
Apple Computer, Inc.
(800) MY-APPLE
www.apple.com

Artistic Appliques- no contact info
Autumn Leaves
(800) 588-6707
www.autumnleaves.com
A.W. Cute
(877) 560-6943
www.awcute.com
Basic Grey™
(801) 451-6006
www.basicgrey.com
Beadery®, The
(401) 539-2432
www.thebeadery.com
Berwick Offray, LLC
(800) 344-5533
www.offray.com
Bo-Bunny Press
(801) 771-4010
www.bobunny.com
Boxer Scrapbook Productions
(503) 625-0455
www.boxerscrapbooks.com
Clearsnap, Inc.
(360) 293-6634
www.clearsnap.com
Clorox Company, The
(510) 217-7000
www.thecloroxcompany.com
Clover Needlecraft, Inc.
www.clover-usa.com
Club Scrap™, Inc.
(888) 634-9100
www.clubscrap.com
Coronado Island Stamping
(619) 477-8900
www.cistamping.com

About the Author Combining a lifelong passion for all things artistic with a love of writing, Kelly Angard brings her own sense of style and sensibility to her scrapbook art. Her professional experience in the creative arts industries includes four years as a magazine writer and editor, twelve years with her own graphic design business—where she created materials for companies such as Disney, Fox TV and Marriott Hotels—and over nine years teaching scrapbook and art classes.

Kelly has worked as a freelance artist and writer for *Memory Makers* magazine and Memory Makers Books, writing a number of articles and books, and creating over 100 pieces of published art.

She lives in beautiful Colorado with her husband David; children, Rachel and Jake, and more pets than she ever thought she'd have. She is currently working on her next project, The Crafty-Girl's Guide and can be reached at www.creativecollage.blogspot.com

Cousin Corporation of America, CCA®
(800) 366-2687
www.cousin.com
Creative Imaginations
(800) 942-6487
www.cigift.com
Creative Memories®
(800) 468-9335
www.creativememories.com
Cruddas Innovations
www.cruddas4innovation.co.uk
C-Thru® Ruler Company, The
(800) 243-8419
www.cthruruler.com
Delta Technical Coatings, Inc.
(800) 423-4135
www.deltacrafts.com
Deluxe Designs
(480) 497-9005
www.deluxedesigns.com
Design Originals
(800) 877-0067
www.d-originals.com
DMD Industries, Inc.
(800) 805-9890
www.dmdind.com
Doodlebug Design™ Inc.
(801) 966-9952
www.doodlebug.ws
Duncan Enterprises
(800) 782-6748
www.duncan-enterprises.com
EK Success™, Ltd.
(800) 524-1349
www.eksuccess.com
Emagination Crafts, Inc.
(866) 238-9770
www.emaginationcrafts.com
Fancy Pants Designs, LLC
(801) 779-3212
www.fancypantsdesigns.com
Far and Away
(509) 340-0124
www.farandawayscrapbooks.com
Fiber Scraps™
(215) 230-4905
www.fiberscraps.com
Fibre-Craft® Materials Corp.
(847) 647-1140
www.fibrecraft.com
Fiskars®, Inc.
(800) 950-0203
www.fiskars.com
Flair® Designs
(888) 546-9990
www.flairdesignsinc.com
Frances Meyer, Inc.®
(413) 584-5446
www.francesmeyer.com
Golden Artist Colors, Inc.
(800) 959-6543
www.goldenpaints.com
Gutermann- no contact info
Heidi Grace Designs
(866) 89heidi
www.heidigrace.com
Helmar®
www.helmar.com.au
Hero Arts® Rubber Stamps, Inc.
(800) 822-4376
www.heroarts.com

Hot Off The Press, Inc.
(800) 227-9595
www.paperpizazz.com
Imagination Gallery, The/Micro Format, Inc.
(800) 333-0549
www.paper-paper.com
Inoxcram- no contact info
Jaquard Products/Rupert, Gibbon & Spider, Inc.
(800) 442-0455
www.jacquardproducts.com
JudiKins
(310) 515-1115
www.judikins.com
Just For Fun® Rubber Stamps
(727) 938-9898
www.jffstamps.com
K & Company
(888) 244-2083
www.kandcompany.com
Keeping Memories Alive™
(800) 419-4949
www.scrapbooks.com
KI Memories
(972) 243-5595
www.kimemories.com
Krylon®
(216) 566-200
www.krylon.com
Li'l Davis Designs
(949) 838-0344
www.lildavisdesigns.com
Lucky Squirrel
(800) 462-4912
www.luckysquirrel.com
Lyra- no contact info
Making Memories
(800) 286-5263
www.makingmemories.com
Marvy® Uchida/ Uchida of America, Corp.
(800) 541-5877
www.uchida.com
McGill, Inc.
(800) 982-9884
www.mcgillinc.com
me & my BiG ideas®
(949) 883-2065
www.meandmybigideas.com
Memories in the Making/Leisure Arts
(800) 643-8030
www.leisurearts.com
Mostly Animals Rubber Art Stamps
(800) 832-8886
www.mostlyanimals.com
Nashua- no contact info
Nature's Pressed
(800) 850-2499
www.naturespressed.com
Nunn Design
(360) 379-3557
www.nunndesign.com
Paper Adventures®
(800) 525-3196
www.paperadventures.com
Paper House Productions®
(800) 255-7316
www.paperhouseproductions.com
Plaid Enterprises, Inc.
(800) 842-4197
www.plaidonline.com

Pressed Petals
(800) 748-4656
www.pressedpetals.com
Prismacolor- see Sanford Corp.
Provo Craft®
(888) 577-3545
www.provocraft.com
PSX Design™
(800) 782-6748
www.psxdesign.com
Quickstick- no contact info
Ranger Industries, Inc.
(800) 244-2211
www.rangerink.com
Robin, Inc.- no contact info
Rubber Stampede
(800) 423-4135
www.deltacrafts.com
Rusty Pickle
(801) 746-1045
www.rustypickle.com
Sanford® Corporation
(800) 323-0749
www.sanfordcorp.com
Saral Paper Corp.
(212) 223-3322
www.saralpaper.com
Scrapbook Wizard™, The
(435) 752-7555
www.scrapbookwizard.com
Scrap Happy- no contact info
Scrappin' Dreams
(417) 742-2565
www.scrappindreams.com
SEI, Inc.
(800) 333-3279
www.shopsei.com
Sharpie- see Sanford Corp.
Speedball® Art Products Company
(800) 898-7224
www.speedballart.com
Staedtler®, Inc.
(800) 927-7723
www.staedtler.us
Stampa Rosa- no longer in business
Stampendous!®
(800) 869-0474
www.stampendous.com
Stamp n' Stuff- no contact info
Stewart Gill Ltd.
www.stewartgill.com
Sticker Studio™
(208) 322-2465
www.stickerstudio.com
Suze Weinberg Design Studio
(732) 761-2400
www.schmoozewithsuze.com
Tsukineko®, Inc.
(800) 769-6633
www.tsukineko.com
Walnut Hollow® Farm, Inc.
(800) 950-5101
www.walnuthollow.com
Xyron
(800) 793-3523
www.xyron.com

Index

Learn more with the authors of these fine titles from Memory Makers Books!

Montage Memories ISBN-13: 978-1-89212-732-7, ISBN-10: 1-89212-732-6, paperback, 112 pgs., #32895

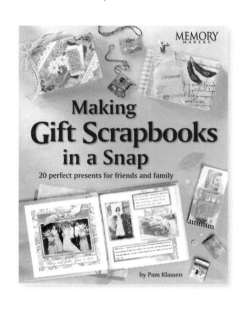

Making Gift Scrapbooks in a Snap ISBN-13: 978-189212-736-5, ISBN-10: 1-89212-736-9, paperback, 96 pgs., #32994

Tags Reinvented ISBN-13: 978-1-89212-747-1, ISBN-10: 1-89212-747-4, paperback, 96 pgs., #33212

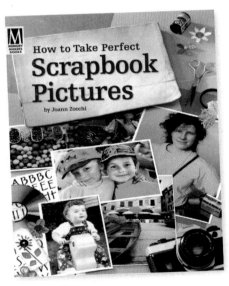

How to Take Perfect Scrapbook Pictures ISBN-13: 978-1-89212-740-2, ISBN-10: 1-89212-740-7, paperback, 112 pgs., #33159

A Passion for Patterned Paper ISBN-13: 978-1-89212-751-8, ISBN-10: 1-89212-751-2, paperback, 96 pgs., #33265

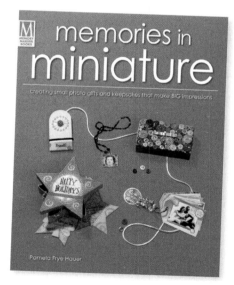

Memories in Miniature ISBN-13: 978-1-89212-750-1, ISBN-10: 1-89212-750-4, paperback, 96 pgs., #33266

These books and other fine Memory Makers Books titles are available from your local art or craft retailer, bookstore or on-line supplier. Please see page 2 of this book for contact information for Canada, Australia, the U.K. and Europe.